CONFIGURING WAREHOUSE MANAGEMENT WITHIN DYNAMICS AX 2012

BY MURRAY FIFE

ISBN-13: 978-1503280915

ISBN-10: 1503280918

Preface

What You Need For This Guide

All the examples shown in this blueprint were done with the Microsoft Dynamics AX 2012 virtual machine image that was downloaded from the Microsoft CustomerSource or PartnerSource site. If you don't have your own installation of Microsoft Dynamics AX 2012, you can also use the images found on the Microsoft Learning Download Center or deployed through Lifecycle Services. The following list of software from the virtual image was leveraged within this guide:

* Microsoft Dynamics AX 2012 R3

Even though all the preceding software was used during the development and testing of the recipes in this book, they may also work on earlier versions of the software with minor tweaks and adjustments, and should also work on later versions without any changes.

Errata

Although we have taken every care to ensure the accuracy of our content, mistakes do happen. If you find a mistake in one of our books—maybe a mistake in the text or the code—we would be grateful if you would report this to us. By doing so, you can save other readers from frustration and help us improve subsequent versions of this book. If you find any errata, please report them by emailing editor@dynamicsaxcompanions.com.

Piracy

Piracy of copyright material on the Internet is an ongoing problem across all media. If you come across any illegal copies of our works, in any form, on the Internet, please provide us with the location address or website name immediately so that we can pursue a remedy.

Please contact us at legal@dynamicsaxcompanions.com with a link to the suspected pirated material.

We appreciate your help in protecting our authors, and our ability to bring you valuable content.

Questions

You can contact us at help@dynamicsaxcompanions.com if you are having a problem with any aspect of the book, and we will do our best to address it.

Table Of Contents

INTRODUCTION

The Warehouse Management module within Dynamics AX is a great feature to configure if you want to do more with your inventory then just track it and count it. When you enable the Warehouse Management features you can start taking advantage of the in-built handheld interface, you can start tracking your workers a little more closely and assign work to them, and it also allows you to create rules on how all of the work within the warehouse is performed so that you can start optimizing and refining your warehouse operations.

Along with all of these more advanced warehouse management features, there is also a little bit more planning and setup that you need to do in order to get everything working, but that doesn't mean that you have to over-complicate your system. If you know the basics of the Warehouse Management module, then you can start off by just configuring what you need initially, and then grow out from there as you start refining your processes.

In this guide we will show you how you can easily configure the Warehouse Management module so that you can start using, and also see that it's not that hard to set up either.

CONFIGURING WAREHOUSE MANAGEMENT CONTROLS

Before we start configuring our Warehouses and processes there are a few extra controls that we need to configure that are related just to the Warehouse Management functions.

Configuring Adjustment Types

To start off we will configure our **Adjustment Types** which we will use to perform our warehouse management transactions.

Configuring Adjustment Types

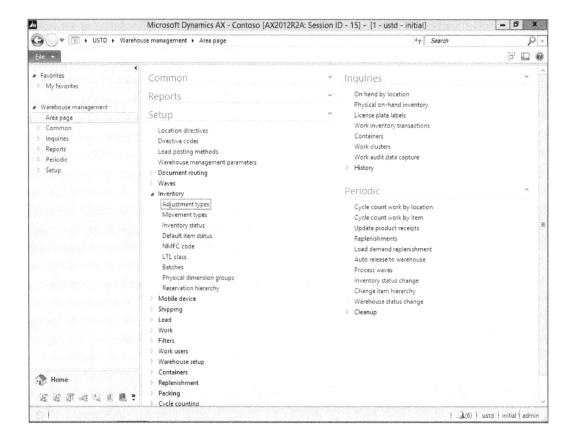

To do this, click on the **Adjustment Types** menu item within the **Inventory** folder of the **Setup** group within the **Warehouse Management** area page.

Configuring Adjustment Types

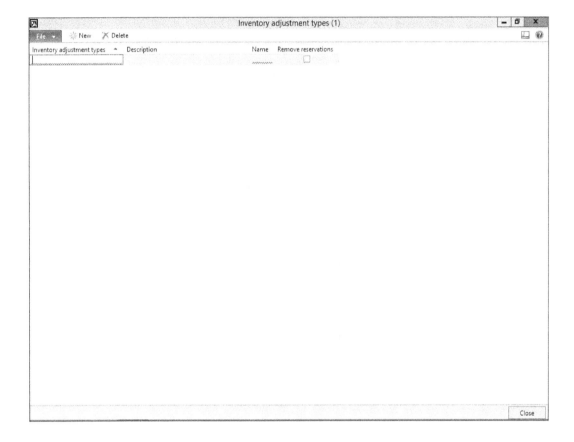

When the **Inventory Adjustment Types** maintenance form is displayed, click on the **New** button in the menu bar to create a new record.

Configuring Adjustment Types

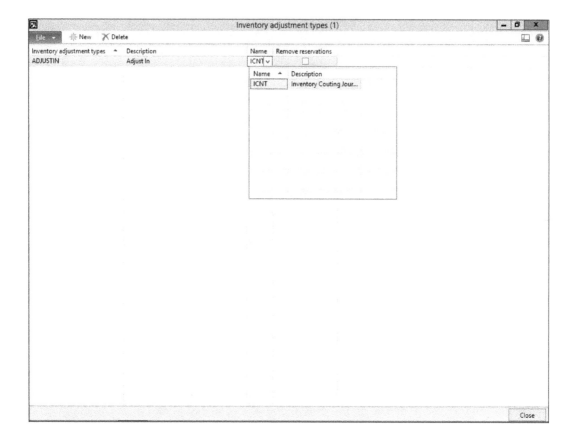

Set the **Inventory Adjustment Type** code to **ADJUSTIN** and the **Description** to **Adjust In**.

Then from the **Name** dropdown box, select the **ICNT** inventory journal code to identify the journal code that will be used for this inventory adjustment type.

Configuring Adjustment Types

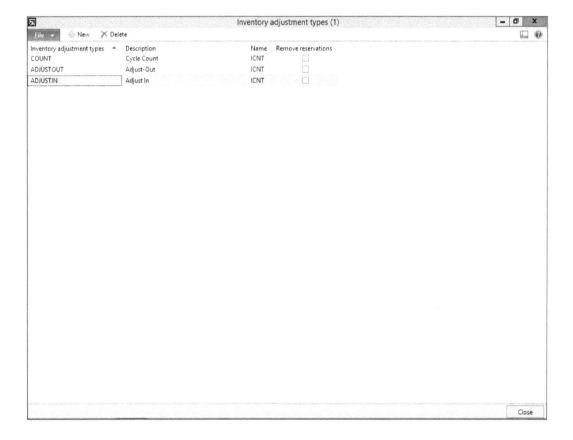

Click on the **New** button in the menu bar to create another record, and set the **Inventory Adjustment Type** to **ADJUSTOUT**, the **Description** to **Adjust Out** and the Journal **Name** to **ICNT**.

Click on the **New** button in the menu bar once more to create another record, and set the **Inventory Adjustment Type** to **COUNT**, the **Description** to **Cycle Count** and the Journal **Name** to **ICNT**.

When you are done, just click on the **Close** button to exit from the form.

Configuring Load Posting Methods

Next we need to configure the **Load Posting Methods**.

Configuring Load Posting Methods

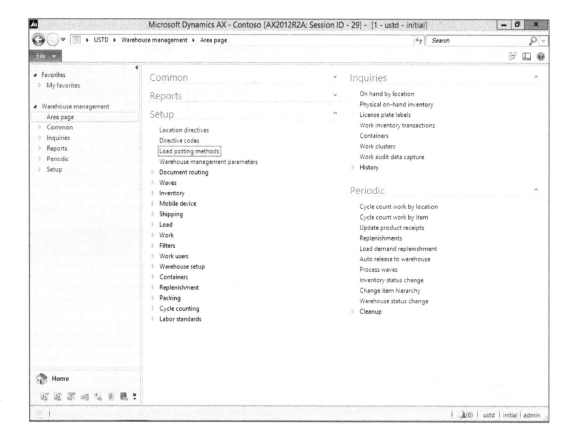

To do this, click on the **Load Posting Methods** menu item within the **Setup** group of the **Warehouse Management** area page.

Configuring Load Posting Methods

When the **Load Posting Methods** maintenance form is displayed, just click on the **Regenerate Methods** button within the menu bar.

Configuring Load Posting Methods

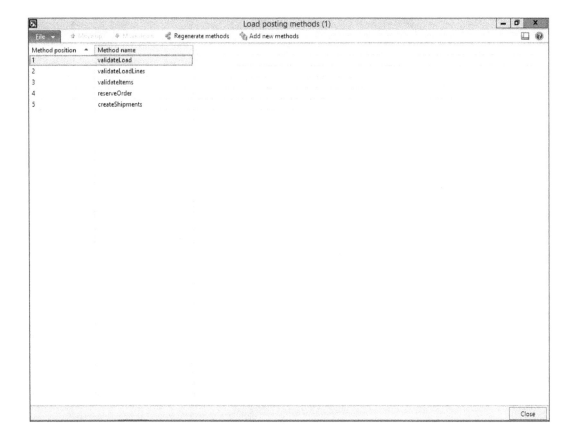

This will automatically create all of the records for you and then you can click on the **Close** button to exit from the form.

CONFIGURING WAREHOUSES

The next step in the setup is to configure your Warehouses. An important point to make here is that you need to create your Sites and Warehouses to be Warehouse Management controlled, otherwise they will just be Inventory controlled, and you won't have access to all of the WMS features.

Configuring A Warehouse Management Enabled Site

The first step is to create a new Site that is enabled for Warehouse Management.

Configuring A Warehouse Management Enabled Site

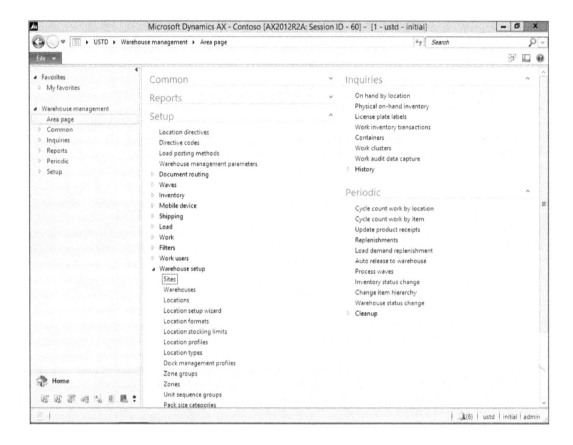

To do this, click on the **Sites** menu item within the **Warehouse Setup** folder of the **Setup** group within the **Warehouse Management** area page.

Configuring A Warehouse Management Enabled Site

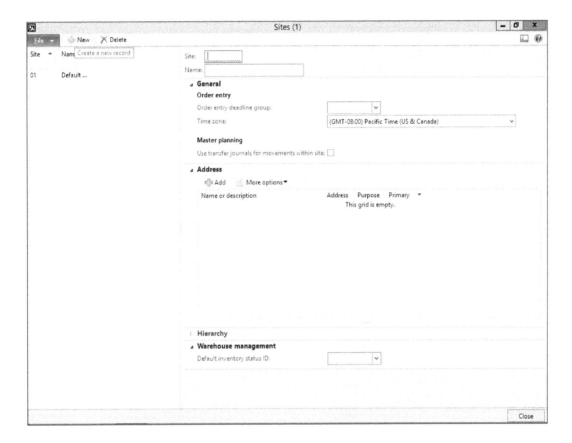

When the **Sites** maintenance form is displayed, click on the **New** button in the menu bar to create a new record.

Configuring A Warehouse Management Enabled Site

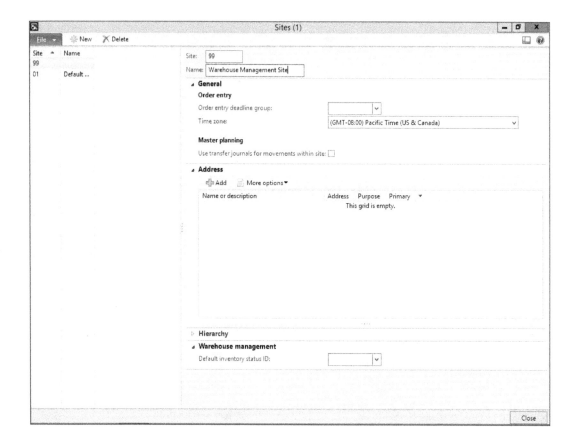

Then assign your new record a **Site** code and also a **Name**.

Configuring A Warehouse Management Enabled Site

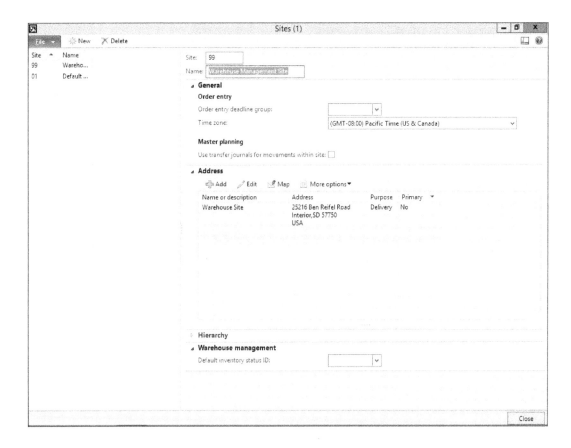

Then click on the **Add** button within the **Address** tab group and add a new **Address** for the main site.

Configuring A Warehouse Management Enabled Site

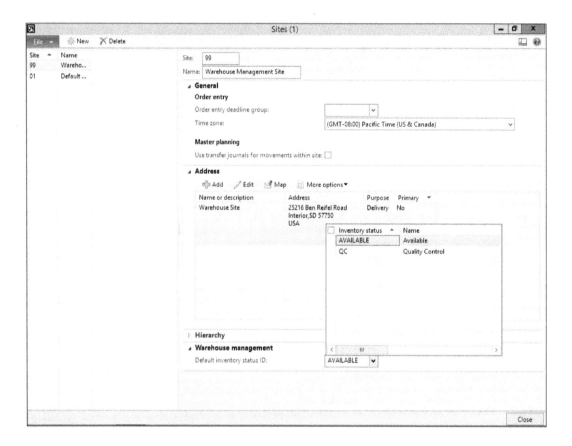

Then click on the **Default Inventory Status IID** dropdown list and select the default inventory status code that you want to use for the site.

Configuring A Warehouse Management Enabled Site

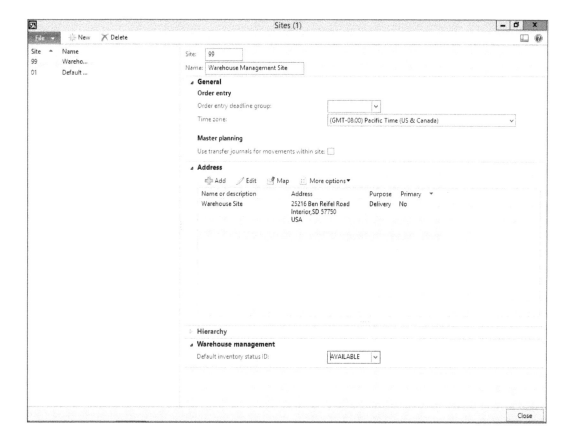

After you have done that, click on the **Close** button to exit from the form.

Configuring A Warehouse Management Enabled Warehouse

Now that we have a Warehouse Management enabled Sire, we can start adding Warehouse Management enabled Warehouses.

Configuring A Warehouse Management Enabled Warehouse

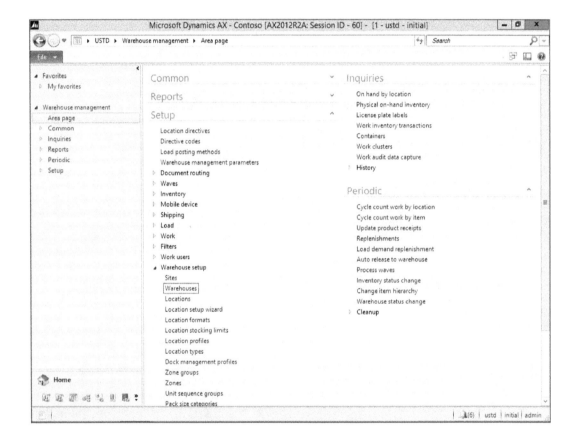

To do this, click on the **Warehouses** menu item within the **Warehouse Setup** folder of the **Setup** group within the **Warehouse Management** area page.

Configuring A Warehouse Management Enabled Warehouse

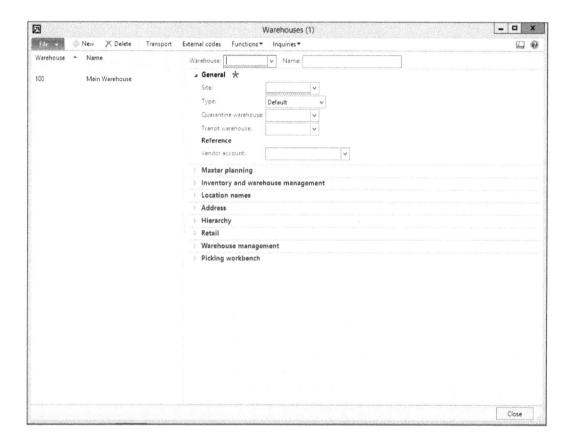

When the **Warehouses** maintenance form is displayed, click on the **New** button within the menu bar to create a new record.

Configuring A Warehouse Management Enabled Warehouse

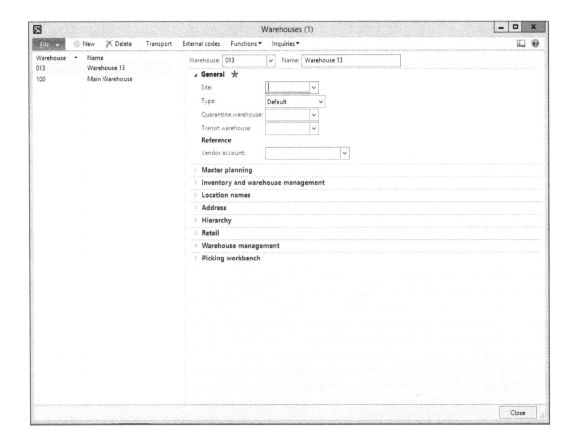

Assign your new record a **Warehouse** code, and also **Name**.

Configuring A Warehouse Management Enabled Warehouse

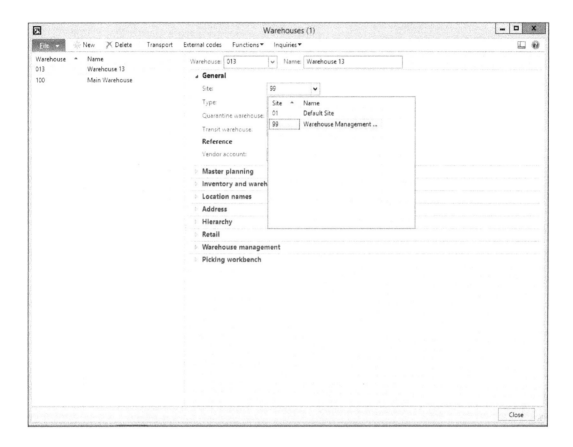

And then select your Warehouse Management enabled **Site** from the dropdown list.

Configuring A Warehouse Management Enabled Warehouse

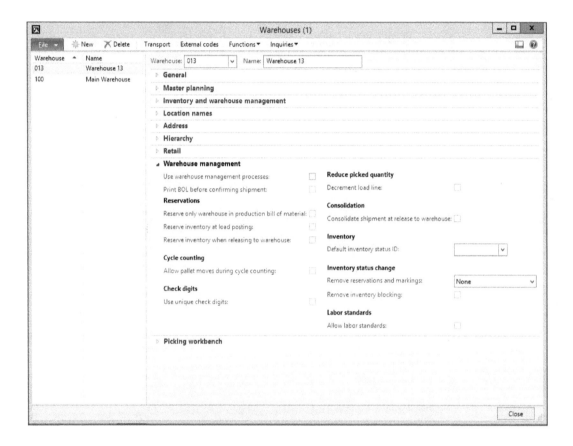

Then expand out the **Warehouse Management** tab group so that you can see all of the warehouse management parameters and controls.

Configuring A Warehouse Management Enabled Warehouse

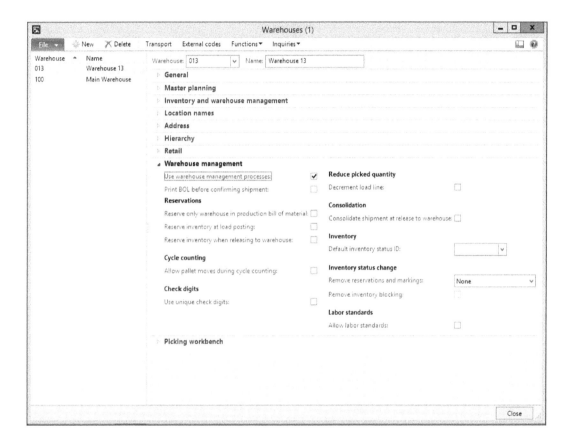

Check the **Use Warehouse Management Processes** check box to identify that the warehouse is to use the WMS features rather than the traditional inventory control functions.

Configuring A Warehouse Management Enabled Warehouse

Then select the **Default Inventory Status ID** that you want all of your inventory to use within the warehouse.

Configuring A Warehouse Management Enabled Warehouse

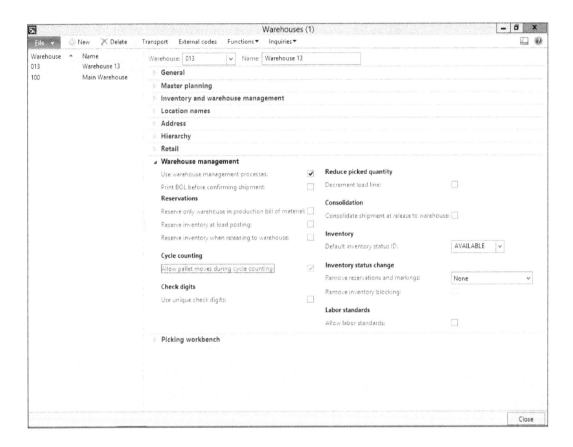

Finally, check the **Allow Pallet Moves During Cycle Counting** flag so that your products won't be frozen during cycle counts.

After you have done that, click on the **Close** button to exit from the form.

Configuring Location Types

Now that we have our warehouse set up, we can start configuring the locations within the warehouse. The first step in doing this is to configure the **Location Types** that you will be using. By setting these up, later on we will be able to have rules based on the locations that specify where we pick and put away products.

Configuring Location Types

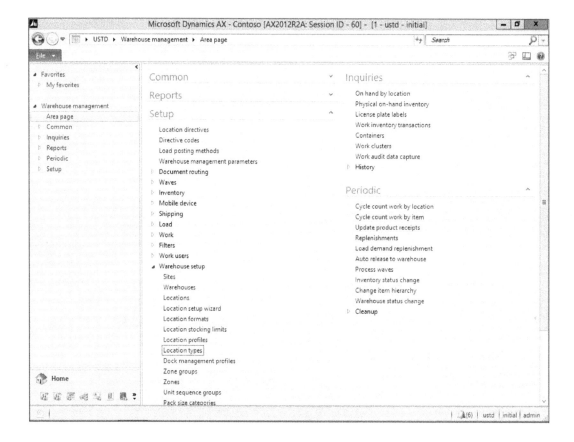

To do this, click on the **Location Types** menu item within the **Warehouse Setup** folder of the **Setup** group within the **Warehouse Management** area page.

Configuring Location Types

When the **Location Types** maintenance form is displayed, click on the **New** button to add a new record.

Configuring Location Types

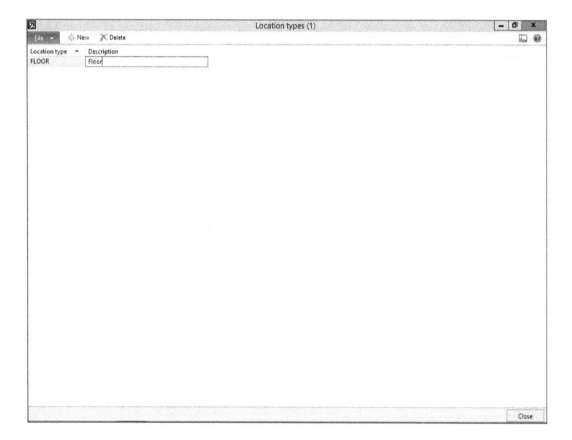

Then set the **Location Type** to **FLOOR** and the **Description** to **Floor**.

Configuring Location Types

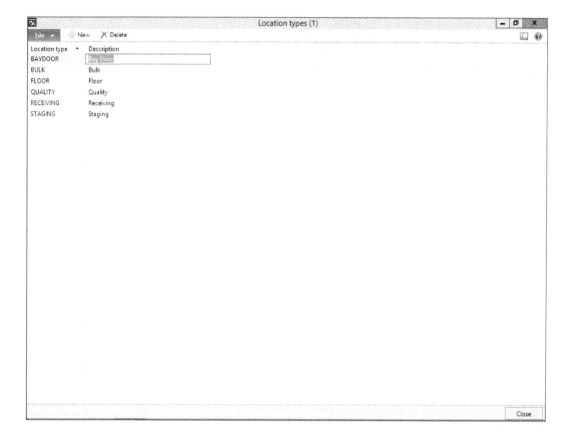

Repeat the process to add in all of the other **Location Types** that you want to track within your warehouse.

After you have done that, click on the **Close** button to exit from the form.

Configuring Location Formats

Next we will want to configure the **Location Formats** which will be used to create our locations. Every location type that we configured is able to have it's own **Location Format** which allows us to model our warehouse locations based on their physical dimensions. i.e. racks may have multiple levels, while floor locations are just single dimensioned.

Configuring Location Formats

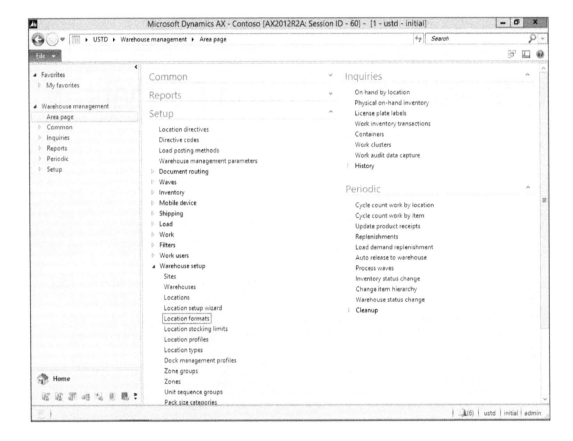

To do this, click on the **Location Formats** menu item within the **Warehouse Setup** folder of the **Setup** group within the **Warehouse Management** area page.

Configuring Location Formats

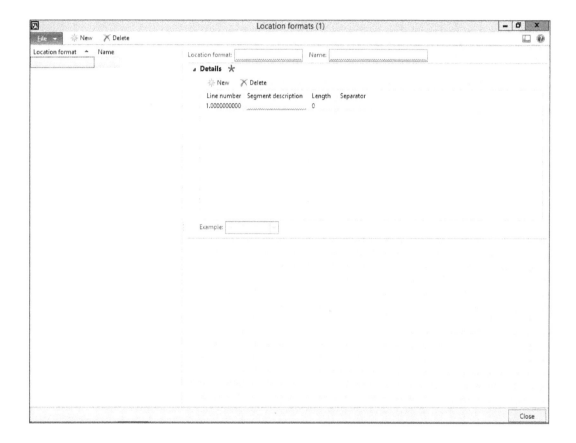

When the **Warehouse Formats** maintenance form is displayed, click on the **New** button in the menu bar to create a new record.

Configuring Location Formats

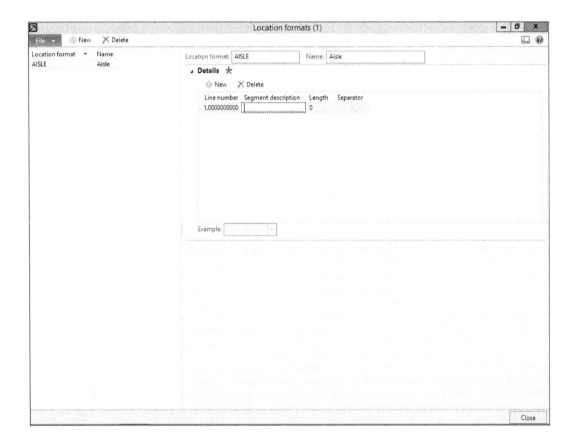

Then set the **Location Format** code to **AISLE** and the **Name** to **Aisle**.

Configuring Location Formats

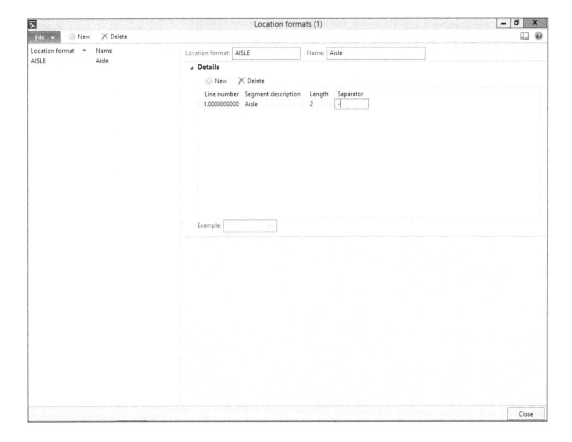

Within the **Details** tab group you will notice that the segments are editable. Set the first **Segment Description** to **Aisle**, the **Length** to **2** characters and then add a **Separator** code to -.

Configuring Location Formats

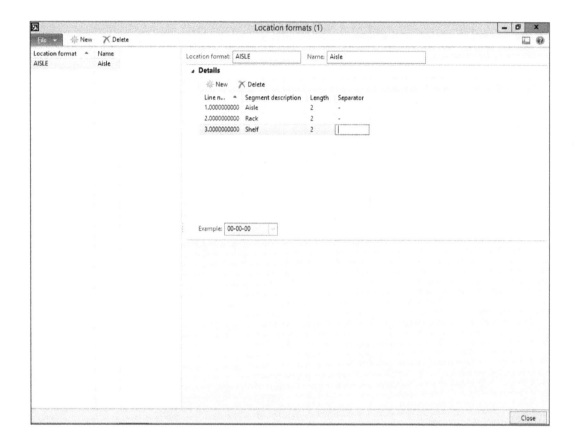

Click on the **New** button within the **Details** tab group to create a new segment and Set the first **Segment Description** to **Rack**, the **Length** to **2** characters and then add a **Separator** code to -.

Click on the **New** button within the **Details** tab group one more time to create a new segment and Set the first **Segment Description** to **Shelf**, and the **Length** to **2** characters.

Configuring Location Formats

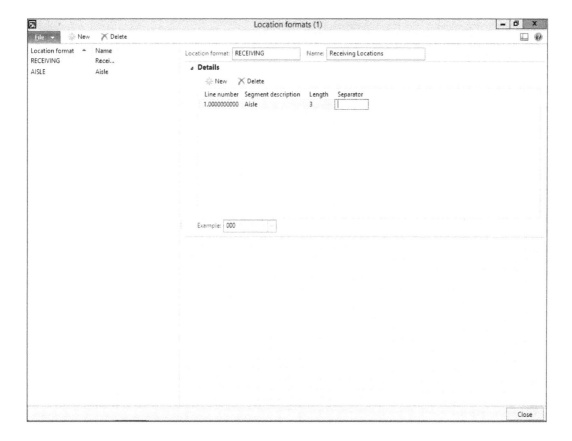

Click on the **New** button in the menu bar to create a another **Location Format** record, set the **Location Format** code to **RECEIVING** and the **Name** to **Receiving Location.**

Then click on the **New** button within the **Details** tab group to create a new segment and Set the first **Segment Description** to **Aisle**, and the **Length** to **3** characters.

Configuring Location Formats

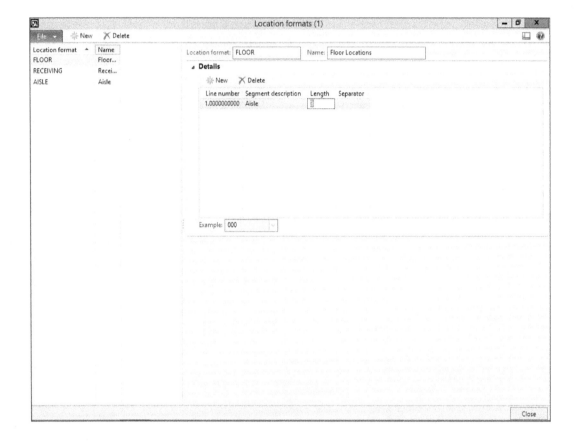

Click on the **New** button in the menu bar to create a another **Location Format** record, set the **Location Format** code to **FLOOR** and the **Name** to **Floor Location.**

Then click on the **New** button within the **Details** tab group to create a new segment and Set the first **Segment Description** to **Aisle**, and the **Length** to **3** characters.

Configuring Location Formats

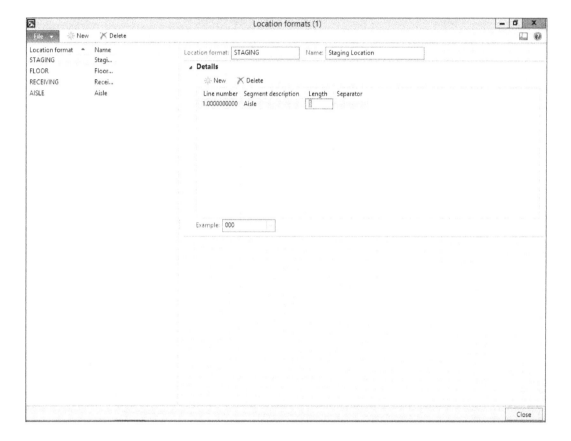

Click on the **New** button in the menu bar to create a another **Location Format** record, set the **Location Format** code to **STAGING** and the **Name** to **Staging Location.**

Then click on the **New** button within the **Details** tab group to create a new segment and Set the first **Segment Description** to **Aisle**, and the **Length** to **3** characters.

Configuring Location Formats

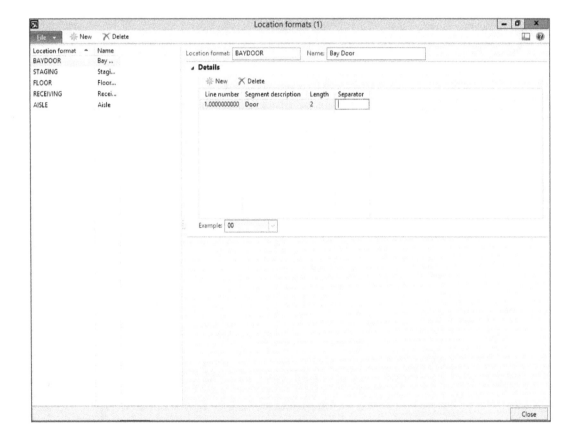

Click on the **New** button in the menu bar to create one last **Location Format** record, set the **Location Format** code to **BAYDOOR** and the **Name** to **Bay Door.**

Then click on the **New** button within the **Details** tab group to create a new segment and Set the first **Segment Description** to **Aisle**, and the **Length** to **2** characters.

After you have set up all of the records click on the **Close** button to exit from the form.

Configuring Location Profiles

Now that we have all of the building blocks for our locations, we can link them together and create our **Location Profiles**.

Configuring Location Profiles

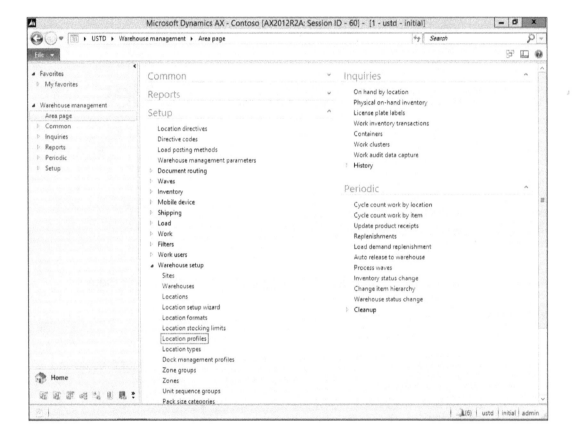

To do this, click on the **Location Profiles** menu item within the **Warehouse Setup** folder of the **Setup** group within the **Warehouse Management** area page.

Configuring Location Profiles

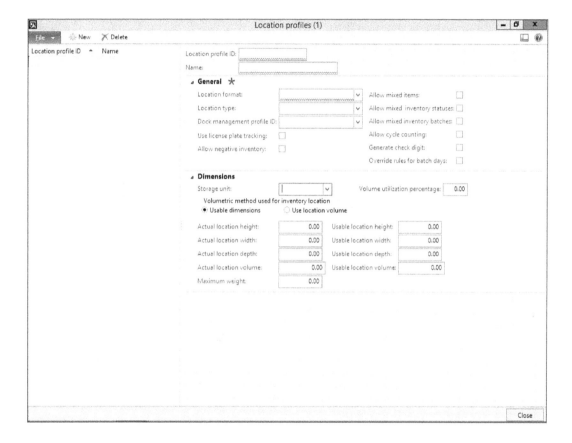

When the **Location Profiles** maintenance form is displayed, click on the **New** button in the menu bar to create a new record.

Configuring Location Profiles

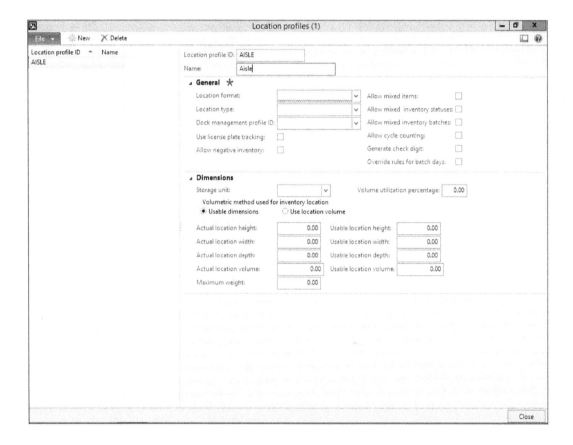

Set the **Location Profile ID** to **AISLE** and the **Name** to **Aisle**.

Configuring Location Profiles

From the **Location Format** dropdown list, select the **AISLE** record.

Configuring Location Profiles

Then from the **Location Type** dropdown list select the **BULK** location type.

Configuring Location Profiles

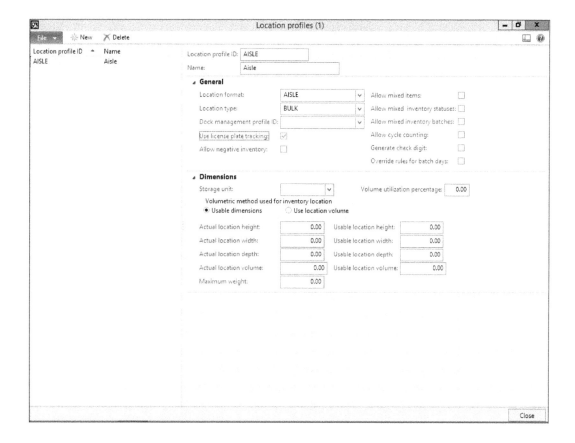

Check the **Use License Plate Tracking** checkbox to enable license plates within the location.

Configuring Location Profiles

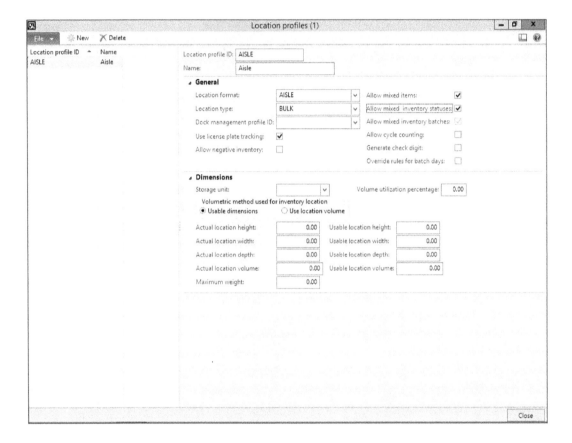

Then check the **Allow Mixed Items** and also **Allow Mixed Inventory Statuses** check boxes to make the location a little more flexible.

Configuring Location Profiles

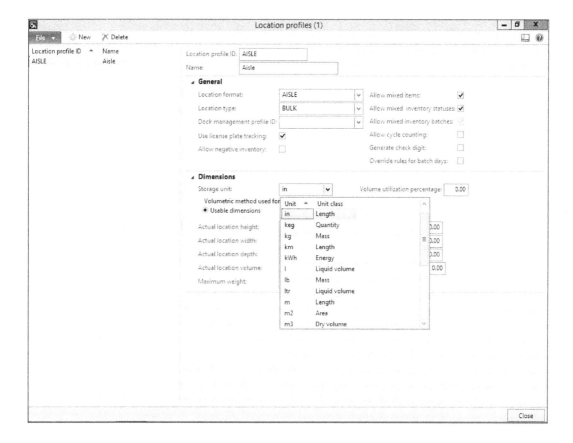

Within the **Dimensions** tab group, select the **Storage Unit**.

Configuring Location Profiles

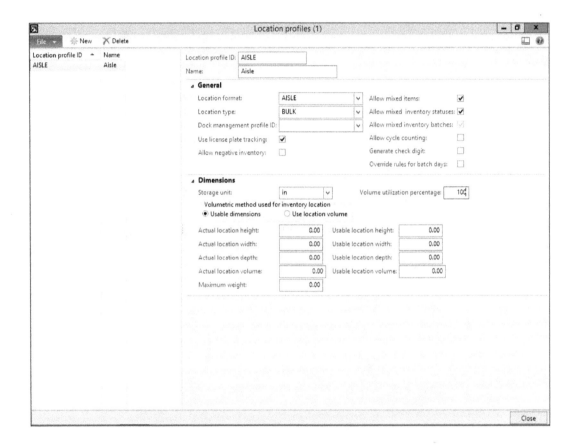

Set the **Volume Utilization Percentage** to **100** to allow us to utilize all the space.

Configuring Location Profiles

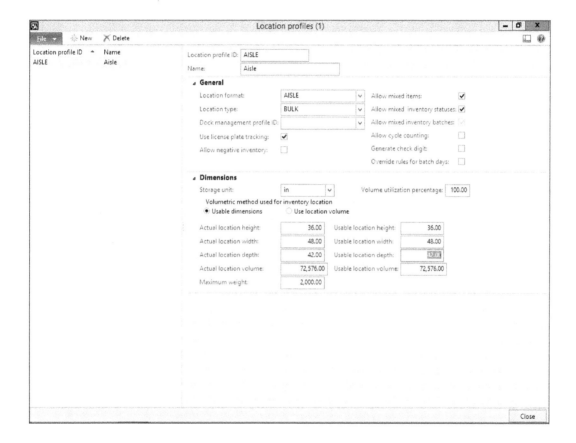

And then set the dimensions of the locations.

Configuring Location Profiles

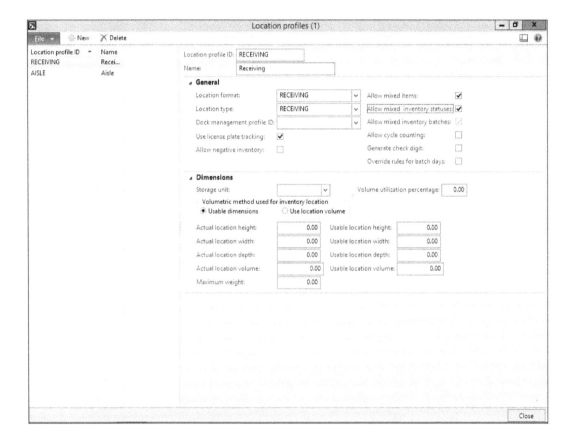

Click on the **New** button in the menu bar to create another record. Set the **Location Profile ID** to **RECEIVING** and the **Name** to **Receiving**. Set the **Location Format** and **Location Type** both to **RECEIVING** and then check the **Use License Plate Tracking**, **Allow Mixed Items** and **Allow Mixed Inventory Statuses** check boxes.

Configuring Location Profiles

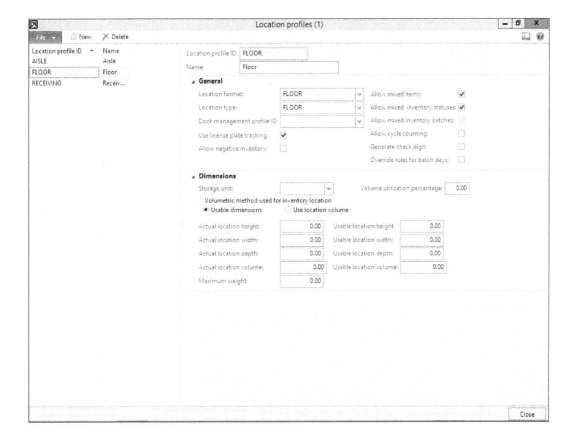

Click on the **New** button in the menu bar to create another record. Set the **Location Profile ID** to **FLOOR** and the **Name** to **Floor**. Set the **Location Format** and **Location Type** both to **FLOOR** and then check the **Use License Plate Tracking**, **Allow Mixed Items** and **Allow Mixed Inventory Statuses** check boxes.

Configuring Location Profiles

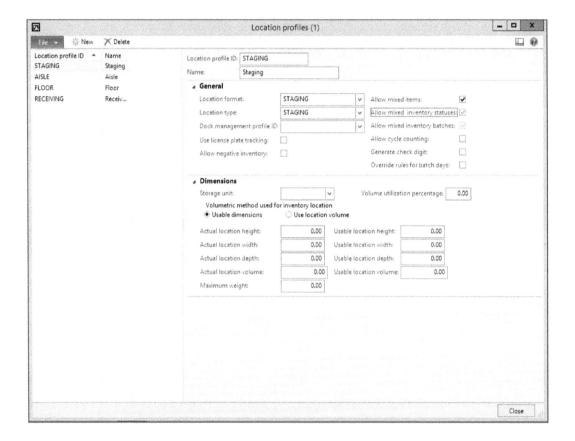

Click on the **New** button in the menu bar to one last record. Set the **Location Profile ID** to **STAGING** and the **Name** to **Staging**. Set the **Location Format** and **Location Type** both to **STAGING** and then check the **Use License Plate Tracking**, **Allow Mixed Items** and **Allow Mixed Inventory Statuses** check boxes.

After you have done this, click on the **Close** button to exit from the form.

Configuring Zone Groups

Now we will start setting up our warehouse zones. Before we do that though we will want to configure some **Zone Groups**.

Configuring Zone Groups

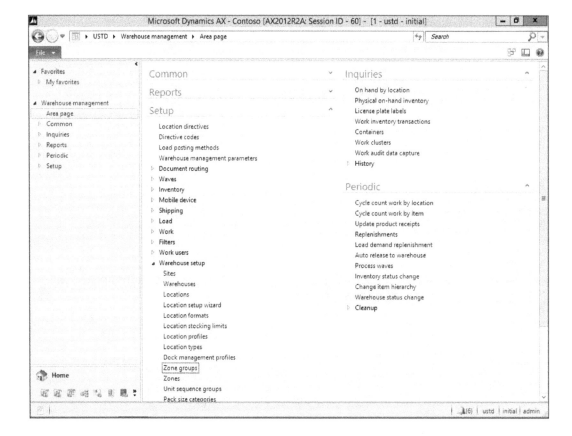

To do this, click on the **Zone Groups** menu item within the **Warehouse Setup** folder of the **Setup** group within the **Warehouse Management** area page.

Configuring Zone Groups

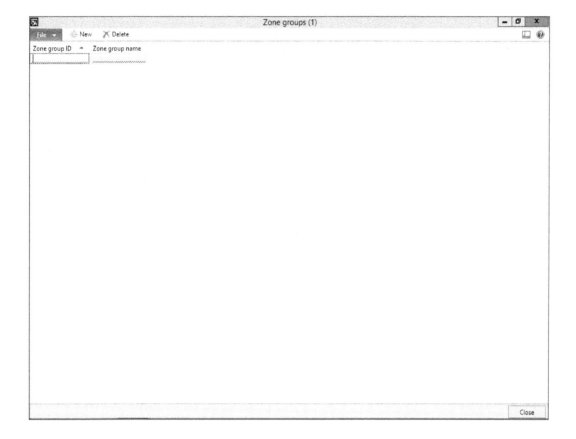

When the **Zone Groups** maintenance form is displayed, click on the **New** button in the menu bar to create a new record.

Configuring Zone Groups

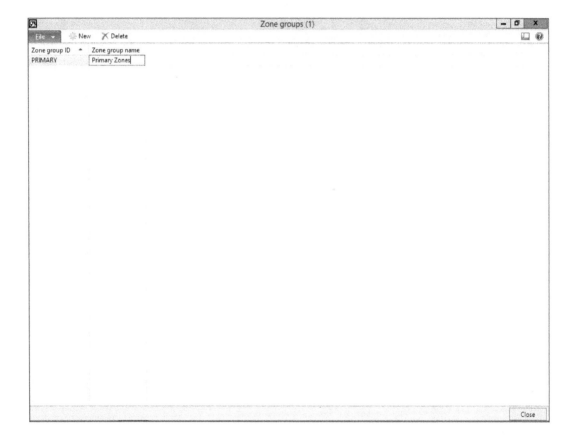

Set the **Zone Group ID** to **PRIMARY** and the **Zone Group Name** to **Primary Zone**

Configuring Zone Groups

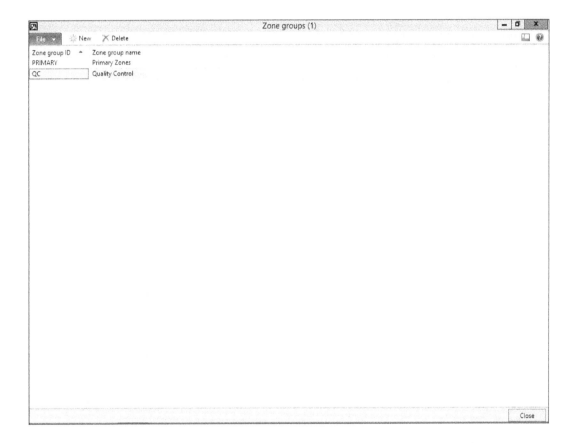

Click on the **New** button once more to create a new record and set the **Zone Group ID** to **QC** and the **Zone Group Name** to **Quality Control**.

When you are done, click on the **Close** button to exit from the form.

Configuring Zones

Once you have configured your zone groups you can set up your warehouse **Zones**.

Configuring Zones

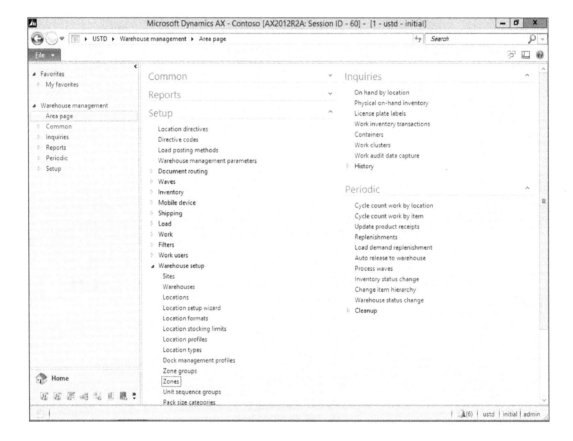

To do this, click on the **Zones** menu item within the **Warehouse Setup** folder of the **Setup** group within the **Warehouse Management** area page.

Configuring Zones

When the **Zones** maintenance form is displayed, click on the **New** button within the menu bar to create a new record.

Configuring Zones

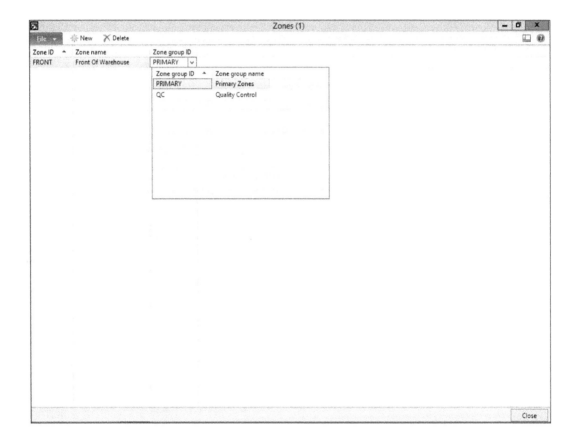

Set the **Zone ID** to **FRONT**, the **Zone Name** to **Front Of Warehouse** and then click on the **Zone Group ID** dropdown list and select the **Primary** record.

Configuring Zones

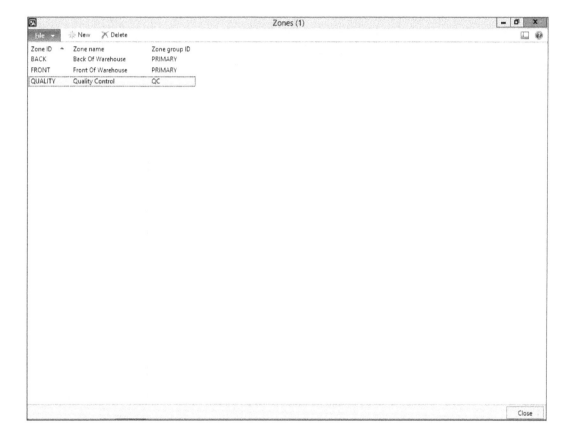

Click on the **New** button within the menu bar again to create a new record and set the **Zone ID** to **BACK**, the **Zone Name** to **Back Of Warehouse** and then click on the **Zone Group ID** dropdown list and select the **Primary** record.

Click on the **New** button within the menu bar once more to create a new record and set the **Zone ID** to **QUALITY**, the **Zone Name** to **Quality Control** and then click on the **Zone Group ID** dropdown list and select the **QC** record.

After you have set up all of the **Zones** click on the **Close** button to exit from the form.

Configuring Receiving Locations

Now we will start building our locations. The first ones that we will set up will be our **Receiving Locations**.

Configuring Receiving Locations

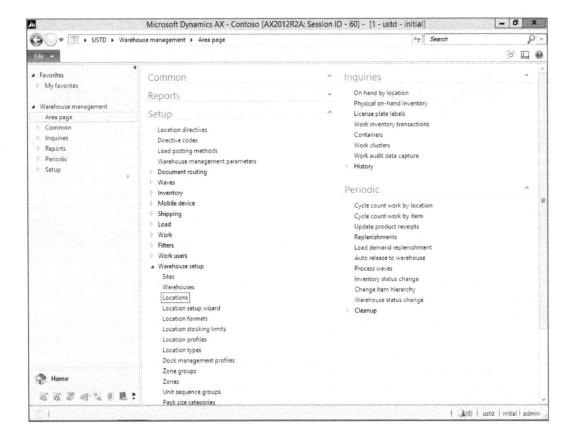

To do this, click on the **Locations** menu item within the **Warehouse Setup** folder of the **Setup** group within the **Warehouse Management** area page.

Configuring Receiving Locations

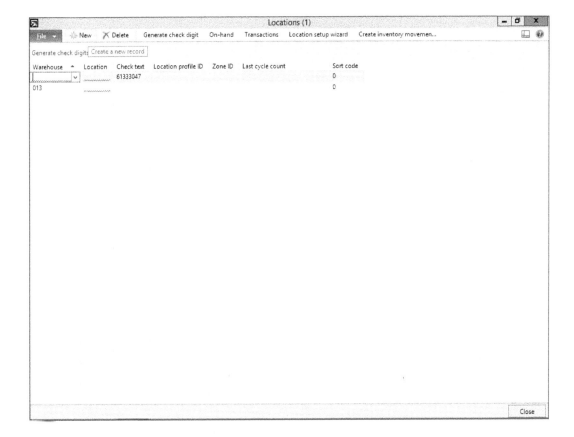

When the **Locations** maintenance form is displayed, click on the **New** button within the menu bar to create a new record.

Configuring Receiving Locations

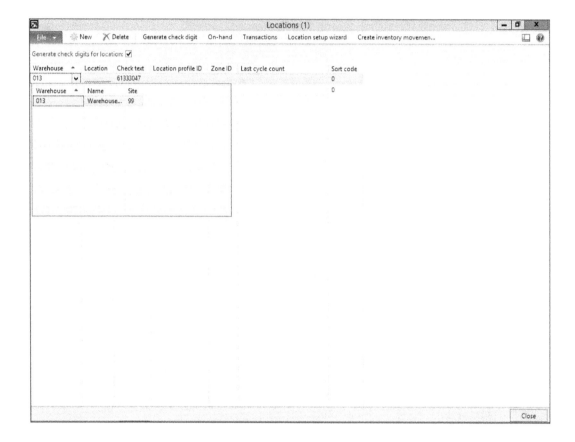

Click on the **Warehouse** dropdown list and select your WMS enabled warehouse.

Configuring Receiving Locations

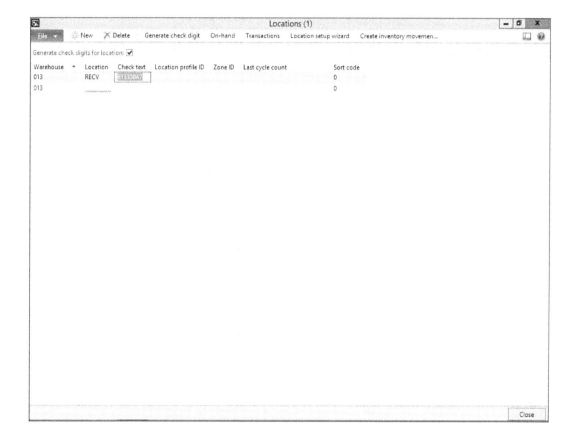

Then set the **Location** to be **RECV**.

Configuring Receiving Locations

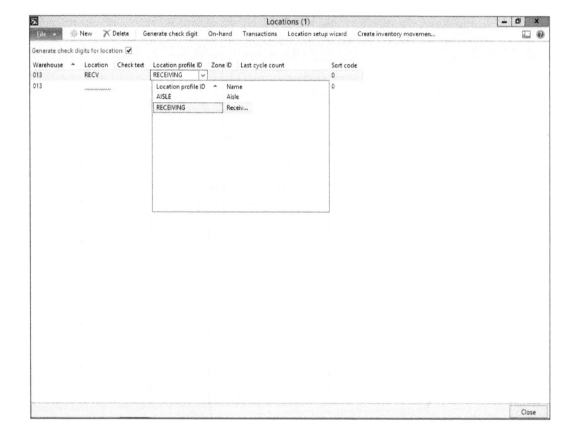

Clear out the **Check Text** field.

Then click on the **Location Profile ID** and select the **RECEIVING** record.

Configuring Receiving Locations

After you have done that you are done.

Configuring Bulk Locations

Next we will create some **Bulk Locations**. Since the bulk locations have multiple aisles, racks and shelves, rather than set them up by hand we will use the **Location Wizard** to create them.

Configuring Bulk Locations

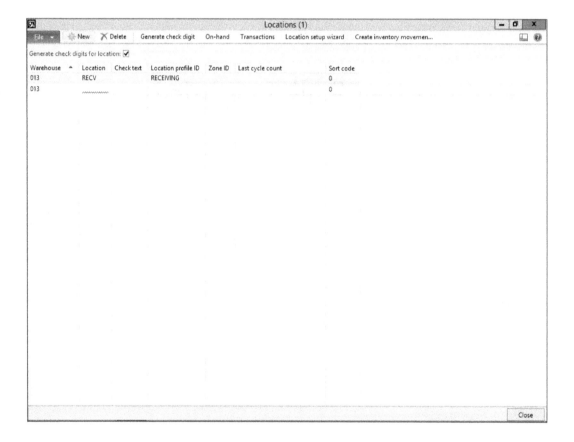

To do this, return to the **Locations** maintenance form, and click on the **Location Setup Wizard** button within the menu bar.

Configuring Bulk Locations

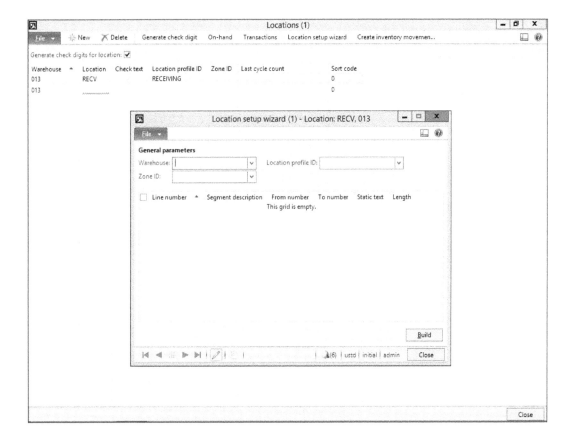

This will open up the **Location Setup Wizard** dialog box.

Configuring Bulk Locations

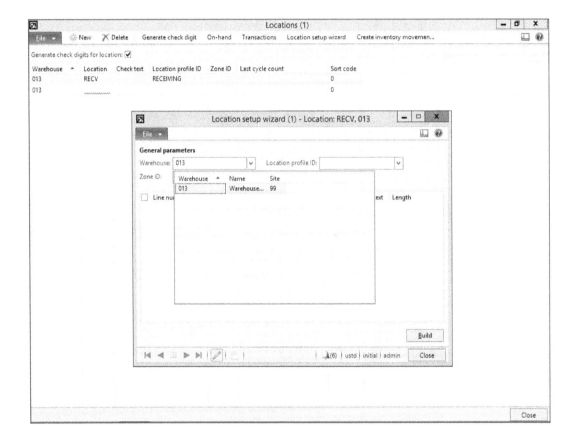

Click on the **Warehouse** dropdown list and select your WMS enabled warehouse.

Configuring Bulk Locations

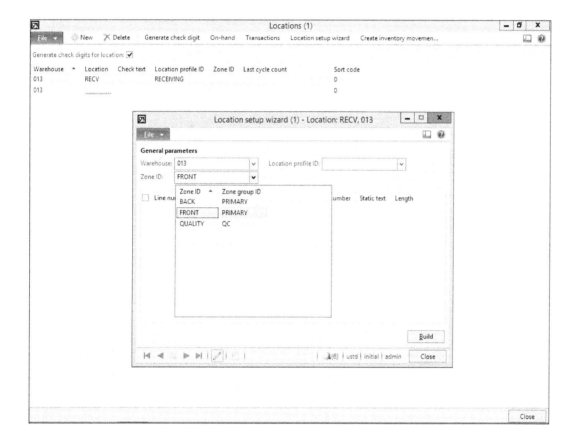

Then click on the **Zone ID** dropdown and select the **FRONT** zone record.

Configuring Bulk Locations

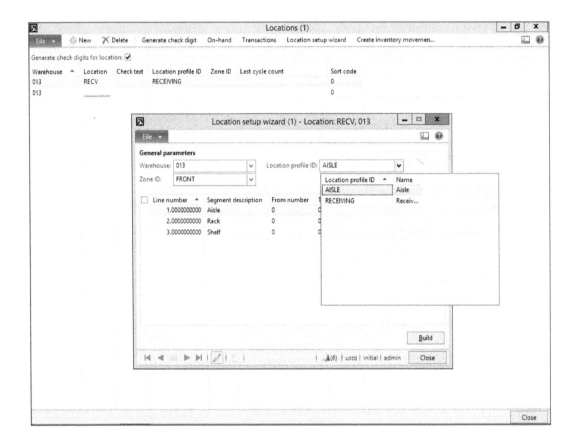

Then select the **AISLE Location Profile ID**.

Configuring Bulk Locations

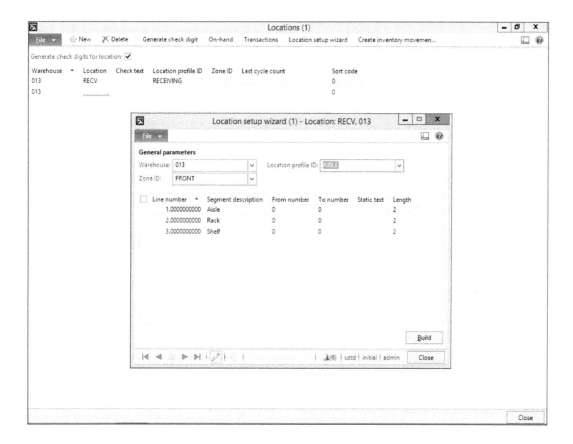

Notice that now the segments are populated on the form.

Configuring Bulk Locations

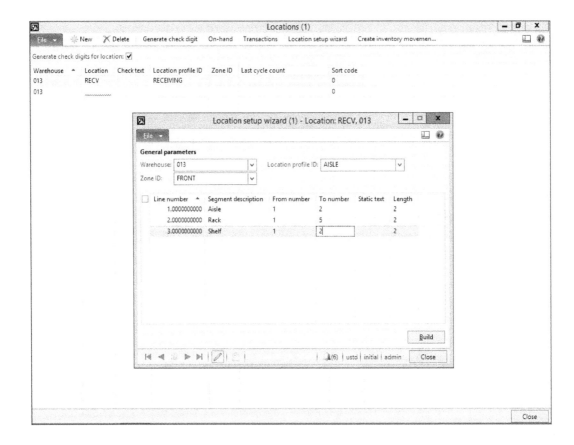

You can change the ranges that you want to create all of the segments for and then click the **Build** button.

Configuring Bulk Locations

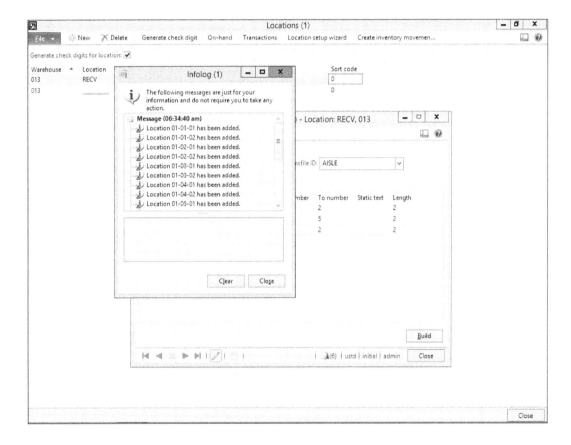

The wizard will give you a notification that the locations have been created and you can close out of the InfoLog, and then click **Close** on the wizard to exit from the form.

Configuring Bulk Locations

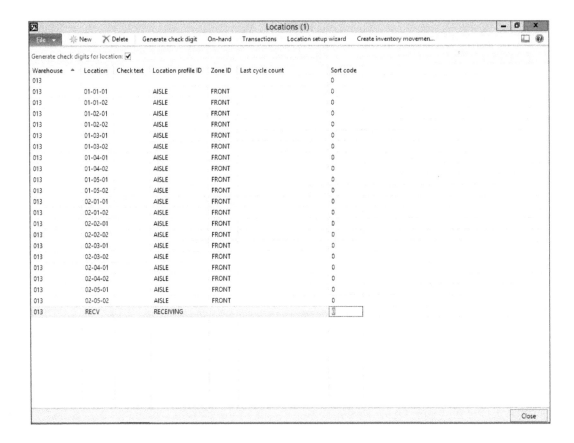

Now you will see that you have a number of bulk locations configured for you.

Configuring Floor Locations

Next we will configure our floor locations.

Configuring Floor Locations

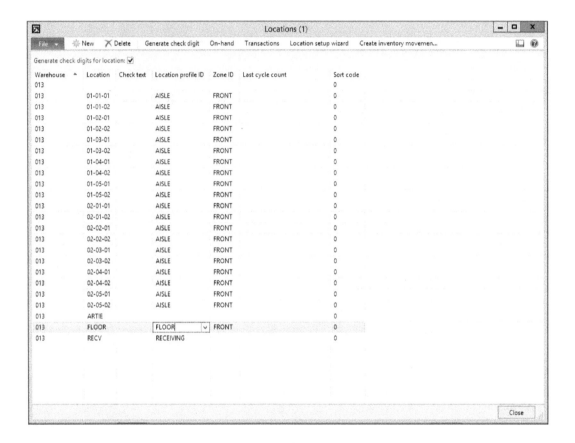

To do this, return to the **Locations** maintenance form, and click on the **New** button to add a new record. Click on the **Warehouse** dropdown list and select your WMS enabled warehouse, and then set the **Location** and **Location Profile ID** both to **FLOOR** and the **Zone ID** to **FRONT**.

Configuring Staging Locations

There is one final location that we need to configure, and that is the **Staging Location**.

Configuring Staging Locations

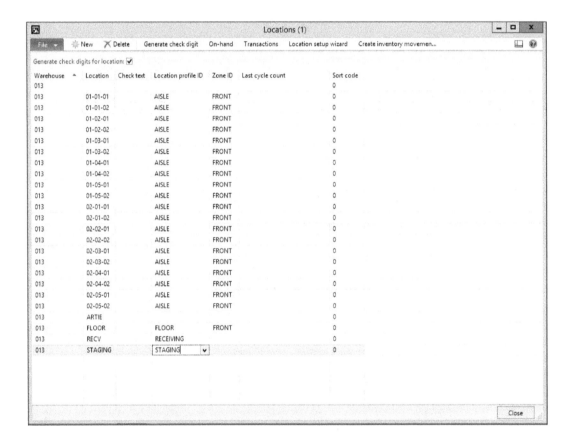

To do this, return to the **Locations** maintenance form, and click on the **New** button to add a new record. Click on the **Warehouse** dropdown list and select your WMS enabled warehouse, and then set the **Location** and **Location Profile ID** both to **STAGING**.

After you have done this, just click on the **Close** button to exit from the form.

Configuring Location Stocking Limits

One final tweak that you may want to configure for your locations is to define the **Location Stocking Limits**, or set them so that the system ignores stocking limits.

Configuring Location Stocking Limits

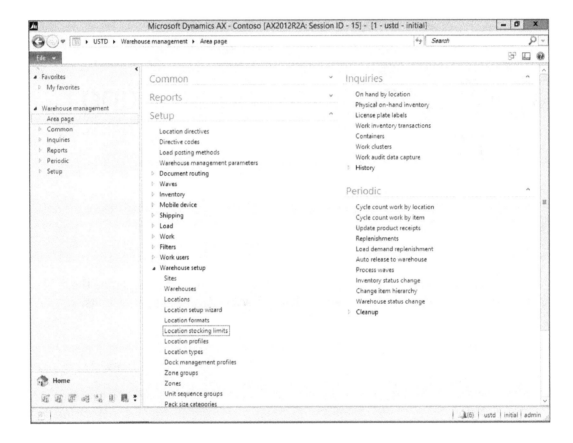

To do this, click on the **Location Stocking Limits** menu item within the **Warehouse Setup** folder of the **Setup** group within the **Warehouse Management** area page.

Configuring Location Stocking Limits

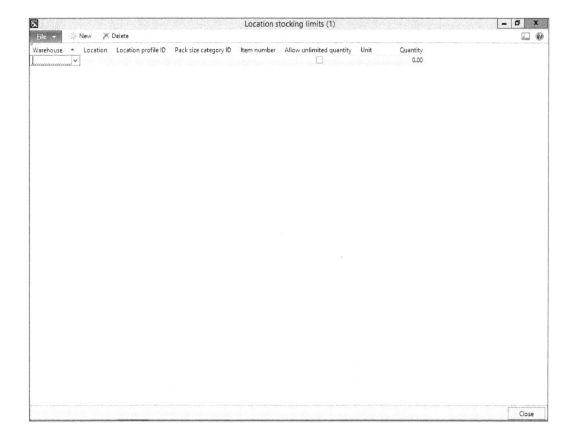

When the **Location Stocking Limits** maintenance form is displayed, click on the **New** button within the menu bar to create a new record.

Configuring Location Stocking Limits

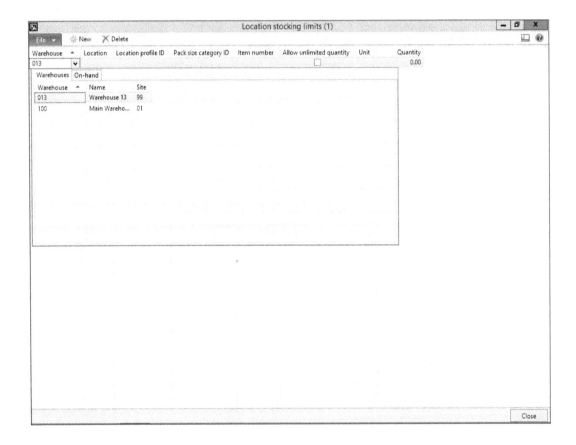

Click on the **Warehouse** dropdown list and select your WMS enabled warehouse.

Configuring Location Stocking Limits

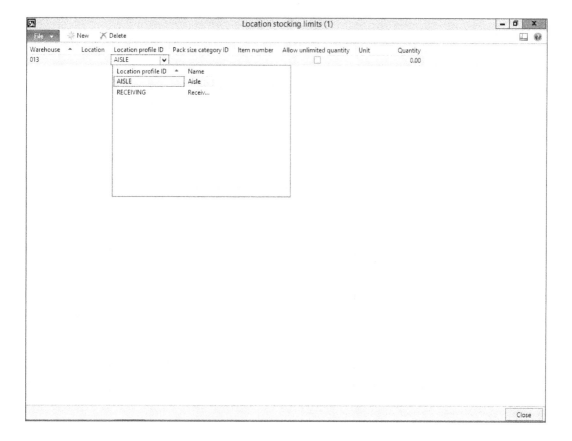

Then click on the **Location Profile ID** dropdown list and select the **AISLE** record.

Configuring Location Stocking Limits

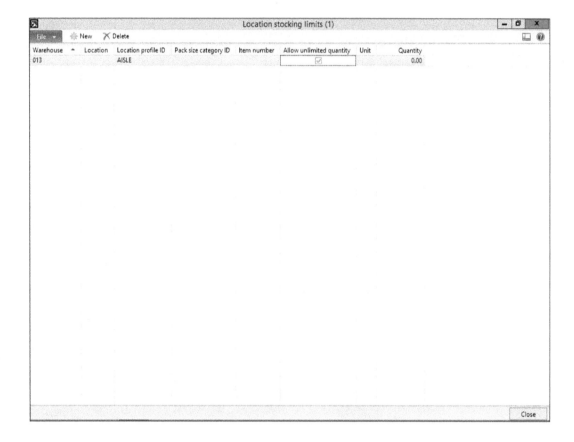

To throw all caution to the wind and not worry about the stocking limits, just check the **Allow Unlimited Quantity** checkbox.

After you have done that, click on the **Close** button to exit from the form.

Viewing Locations Graphically

Once you have configured your locations, you can take a little bit of a breath and see them graphically within the **Location** viewer.

Viewing Locations Graphically

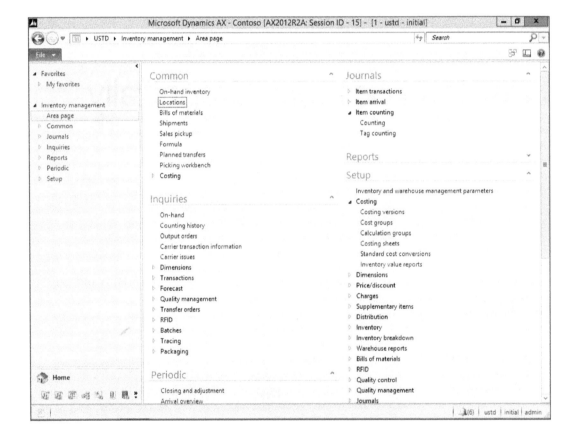

To do this click on the **Locations** menu item within the **Common** group of the **Inventory Management** area page.

Viewing Locations Graphically

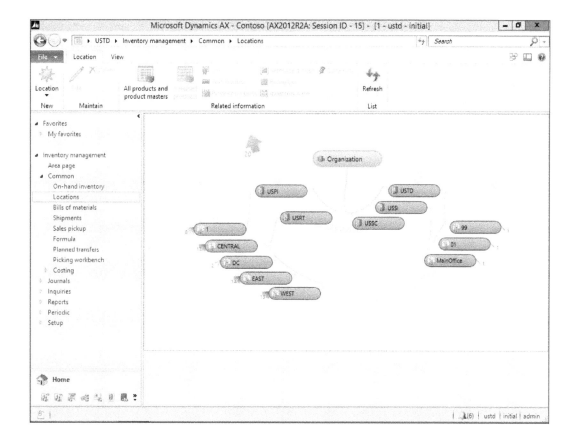

When the **Locations** viewer is displayed you should see your company and new WMS enabled site.

Viewing Locations Graphically

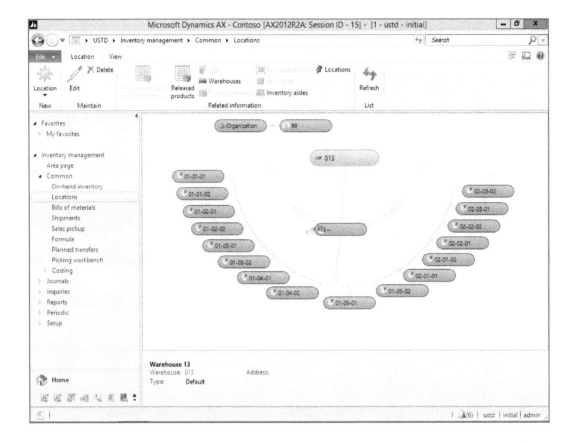

If you drill through into the WMS enabled site you will find your new **Warehouse** and also all of the locations that you configured.

How cool is that?

Updating The Default Warehouse Location

Now that you have configured your warehouse locations, you can return to the **Warehouse** record and tidy up some of the data by setting the default warehouse locartions.

Updating The Default Warehouse Location

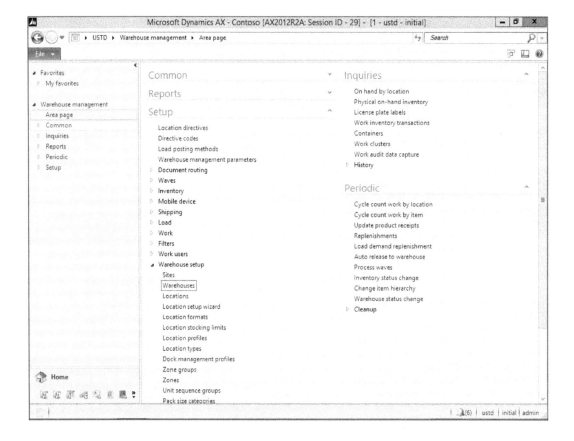

To do this, click on the **Warehouses** menu item within the **Warehouse Setup** folder of the **Set** group of the **Warehouse Management** area page.

Updating The Default Warehouse Location

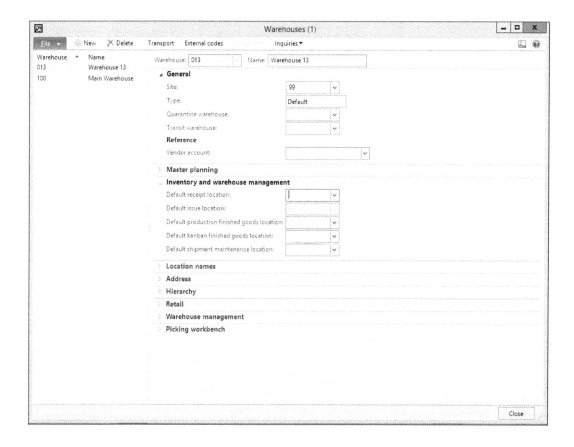

When the **Warehouses** maintenance form is displayed, select your WMS enabled warehouse and then expand the **Inventory And Warehouse Management** tab group.

Updating The Default Warehouse Location

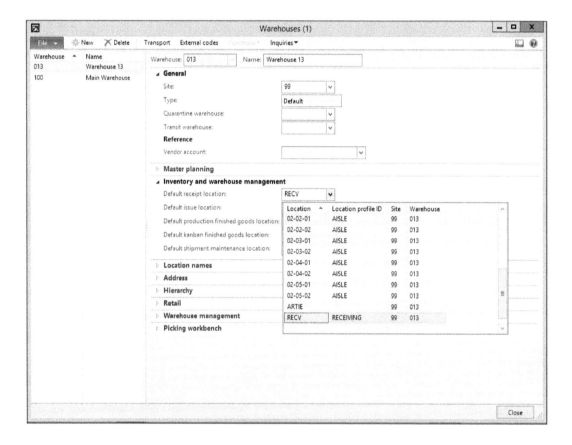

Click on the **Default Receipt Location** dropdown list and select your **RECV** location that you just configured.

Updating The Default Warehouse Location

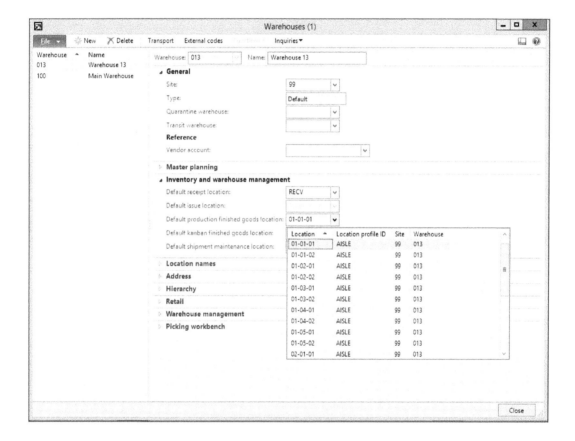

Then select a **Default Production Finished Goods Location** from the dropdown list.

Updating The Default Warehouse Location

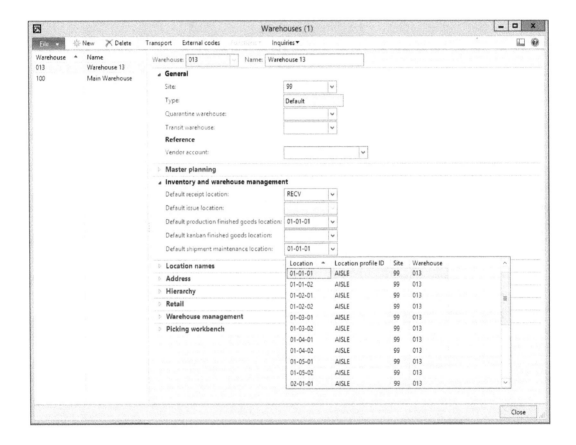

And also select a **Default Shipment Maintenance Location** from the dropdown list.

After you have done that, click on the **Close** button to exit from the form.

Configuring Default Location Profiles

The final step in the configuring of the warehouse is to set some of the default location profiles within the Warehouse Management parameters.

Configuring Default Location Profiles

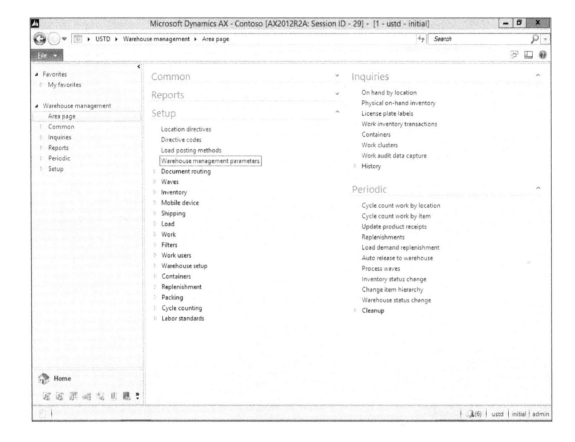

To do this, click on the **Warehouse Management Parameters** menu item within the **Setup** group of the **Warehouse Management** area page.

Configuring Default Location Profiles

When the **Warehouse Management Parameters** maintenance form is displayed, select the **General** page.

Configuring Default Location Profiles

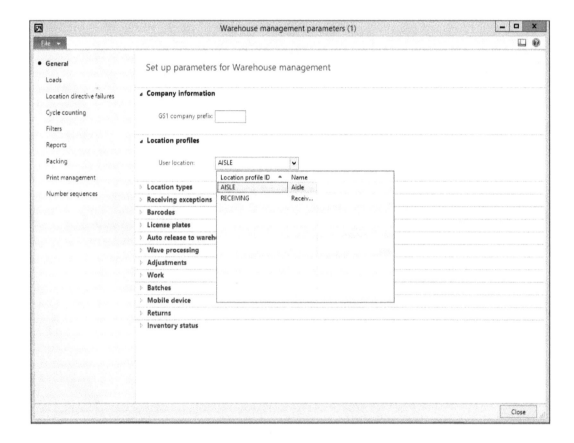

Then within the **Location Profiles** tab group, click on the **User Location** dropdown list and then select the **AISLE Location Profile ID**.

Configuring Default Location Profiles

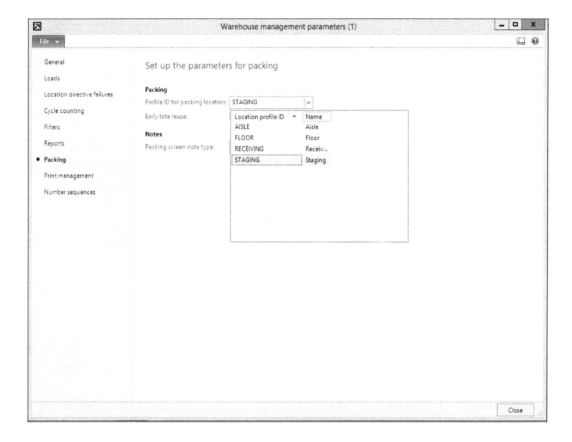

Then switch to the **Packing** page, and select the **STAGING Location Profile ID** from the **Profile ID For Packing Location** dropdown list.

Configuring Default Location Profiles

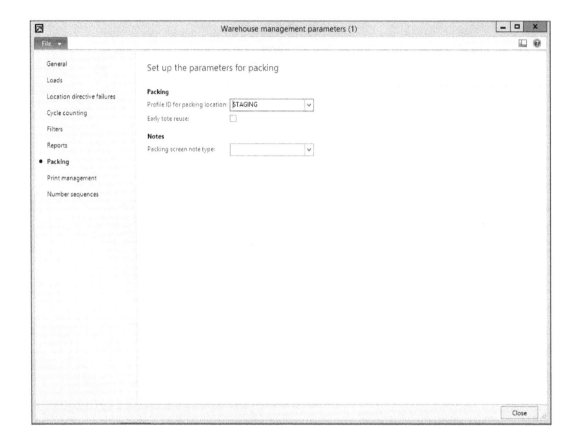

After you have done that, just click on the **Close** button to exit from the form.

CONFIGURING PRODUCTS

Now we will need to configure our products so that they will be recognized by the Warehouse Management functions.

Configuring Unit Sequence Groups

The first tweak that we need to make for the products is to configure some **Unit Sequence Groups**. These are used to convert units of measures based on hierarchies, and every unit of measure that is going to be used in the system needs to be defined here. We are not going to set up all of the units though – just the ones that we need to track in our warehouse.

Configuring Unit Sequence Groups

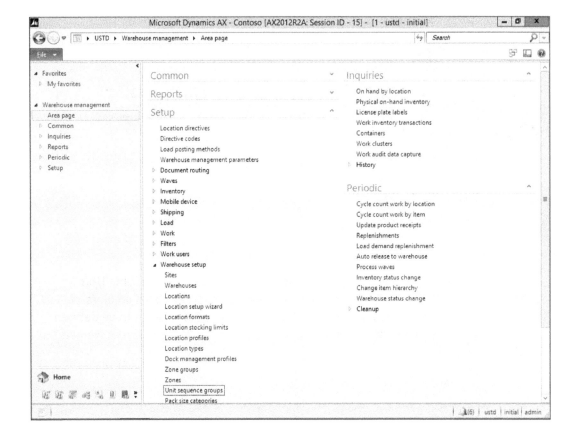

To do this, click on the **Unit Sequence Groups** menu item within the **Warehouse Setup** folder of the **Setup** group within the **Warehouse Management** area page.

Configuring Unit Sequence Groups

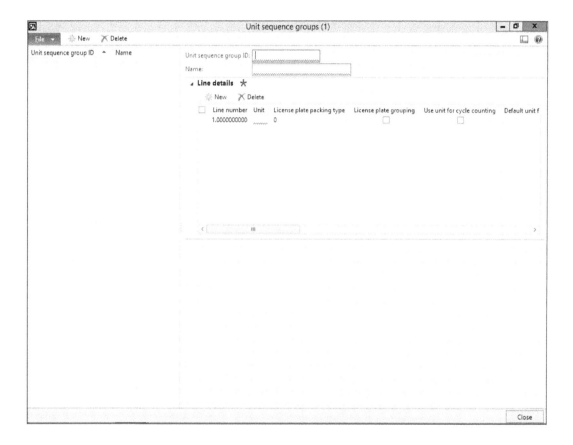

When the **Unit Sequence Groups** maintenance form is displayed, click on the **New** button within the menu bar to create a new record.

Configuring Unit Sequence Groups

Assign your record a **Unit Sequence Group ID** and also a **Name**.

Configuring Unit Sequence Groups

Within the **Line Details** set the **Unit** that you will be using and then check all of the usage flags.

Configuring Unit Sequence Groups

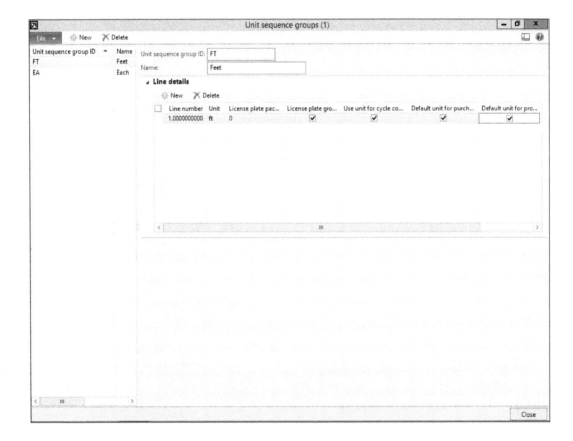

Add any additional units of measure that you will be using and then click on the **Close** button to exit from the form.

Configuring Reservation Hierarchies

Another new control that we need to configure within warehouse management are the **Reservation Hierarchies**. These are used to determine at what level products are reserved at during the sales cycle. For example, you can use these to reserve serialized products at the location level at order entry and only allocate the serial number at the time of shipping.

Configuring Reservation Hierarchies

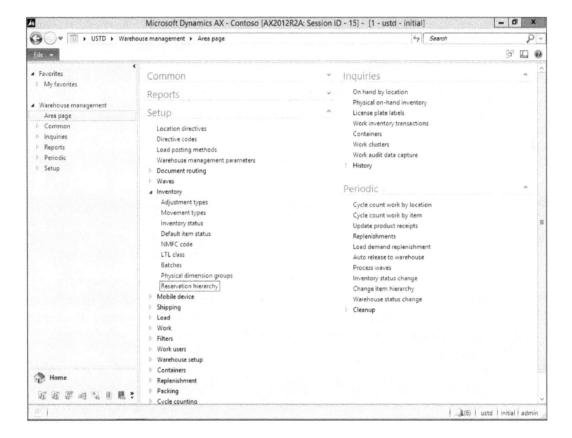

To do this, click on the **Reservation Hierarchy** menu item within the **Inventory** folder of the **Setup** group within the **Warehouse Management** area page.

Configuring Reservation Hierarchies

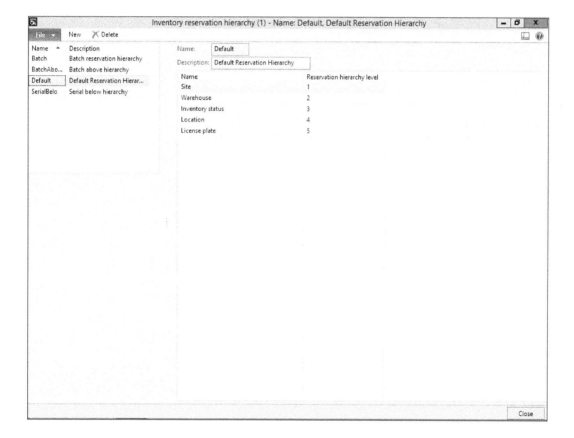

By default, these are already configured.

Configuring A Warehouse Management Enabled Storage Dimension Group

To enable a product to be managed through Warehouse Management, it needs to be assigned a warehouse enabled **Storage Dimension Group**. So the next step in the process is to create a **Storage Dimension Group** that we can use.

Configuring A Warehouse Management Enabled Storage Dimension Group

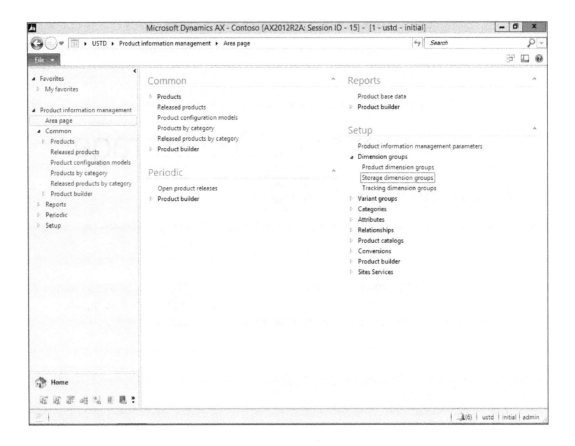

To do this, click on the **Storage Dimension Groups** menu item within the **Dimension Groups** folder of the **Setup** group within the **Product Information Management** area page.

Configuring A Warehouse Management Enabled Storage Dimension Group

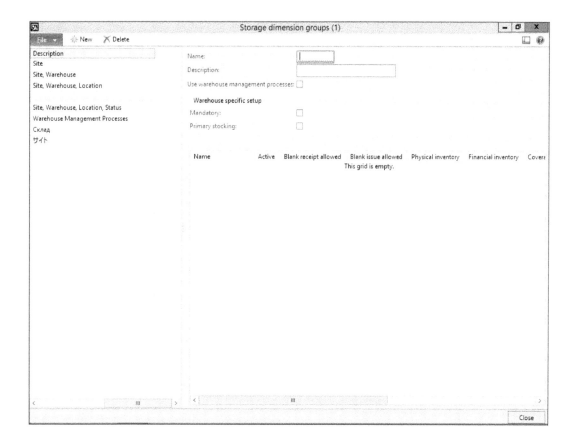

When the **Storage Dimension Groups** maintenance form is displayed, click on the **New** button within the menu bar to create a new record.

Configuring A Warehouse Management Enabled Storage Dimension Group

Set the new records **Name** to **LPN** and the **Description** to be **Site, Warehouse, Location, Status, LPN.**

Configuring A Warehouse Management Enabled Storage Dimension Group

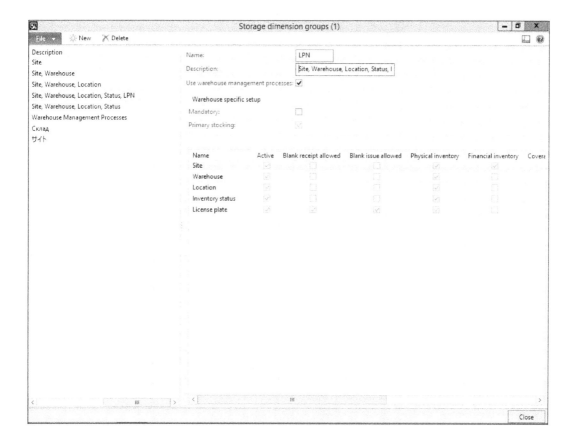

Then check the **Use Warehouse Management Processes** flag on the record.

Configuring A Warehouse Management Enabled Storage Dimension Group

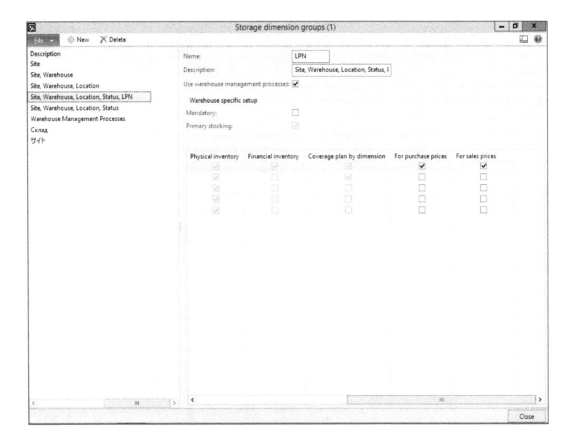

Within the inventory statuses matrix, scroll to the far right and check the **For Purchase Prices** and **For Sales Prices** flags on the **Site**.

Then click on the **Close** button to exit from the form.

Creating A Warehouse Management Enabled Product

Now we have all the information that we need to start configuring our Warehouse Management enabled products.

Creating A Warehouse Management Enabled Product

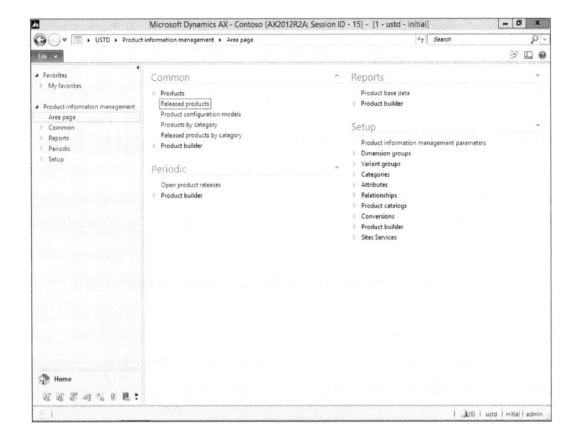

To do this, click on the **Released Products** menu item within the **Common** group of the **Product Information Management** area page.

Creating A Warehouse Management Enabled Product

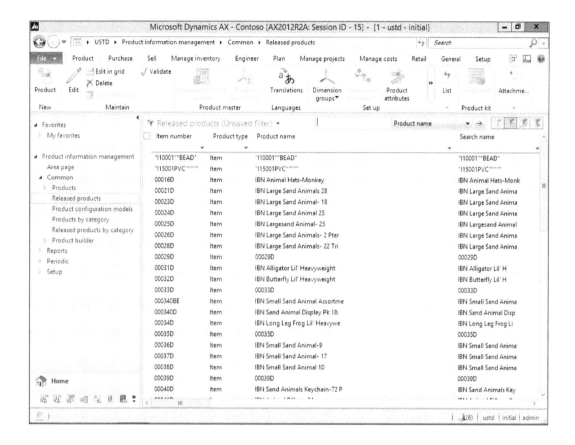

When the **Released Products** list page is displayed, click on the **Product** button within the **New** group of the **Product** ribbon bar.

Creating A Warehouse Management Enabled Product

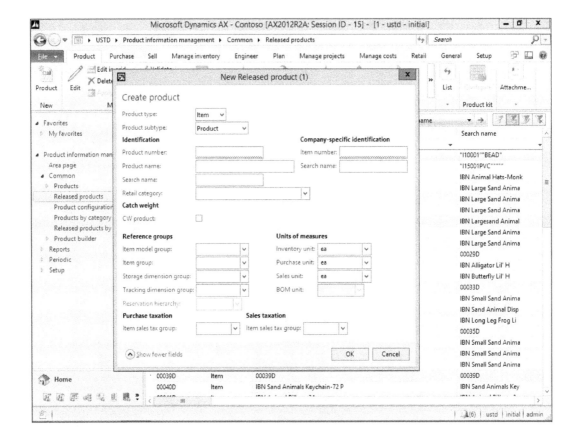

This will open up the **New Released Product** dialog box.

Creating A Warehouse Management Enabled Product

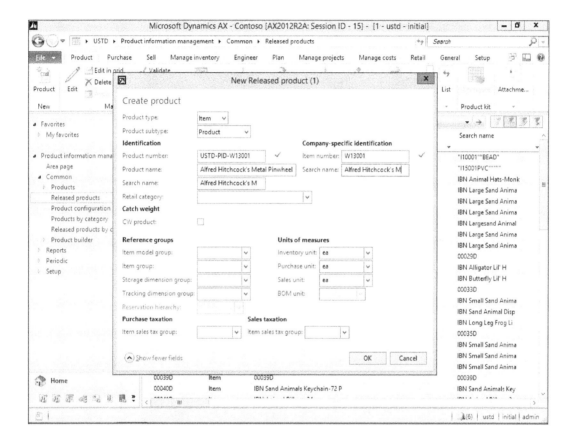

Assign your product a **Product Number**, a **Product Name**, a **Item Number** and also set the **Search Names** for the product and item.

Creating A Warehouse Management Enabled Product

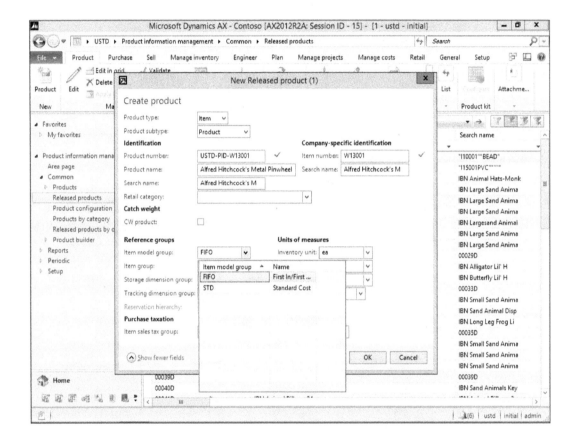

From the dropdown list, select the **Item Model Group** for the product.

Creating A Warehouse Management Enabled Product

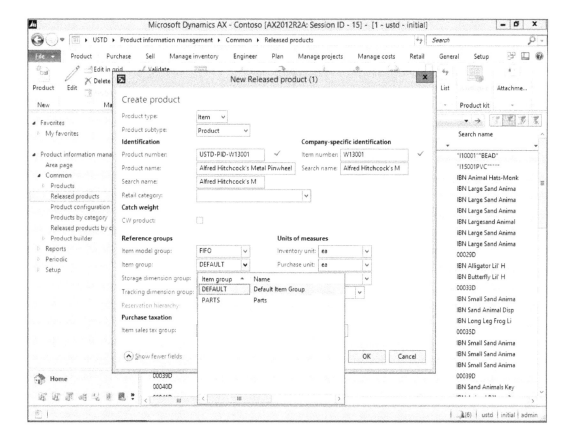

Then select an **Item Group** for the product.

Creating A Warehouse Management Enabled Product

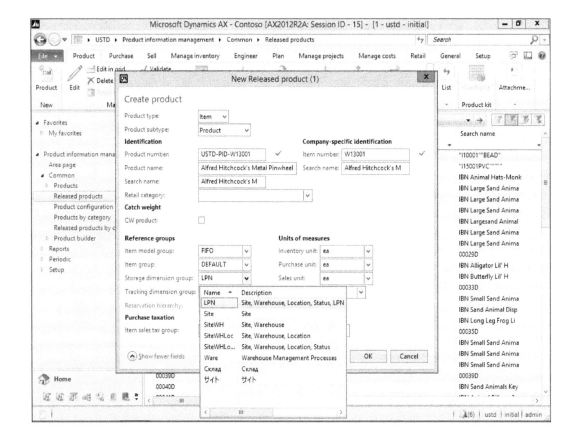

Then assign a **Storage Dimension Group** that is WMS enabled.

Creating A Warehouse Management Enabled Product

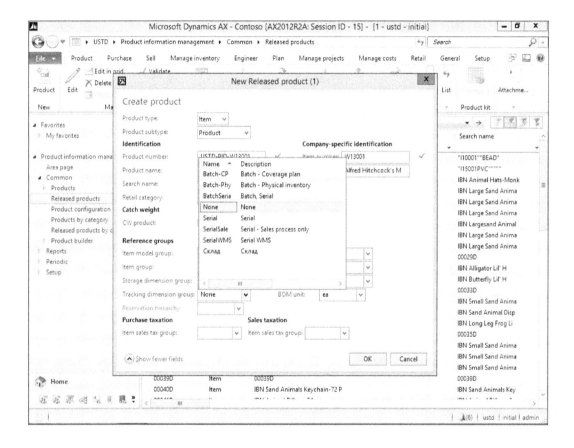

Select a **Tracking Dimension** for your product.

Creating A Warehouse Management Enabled Product

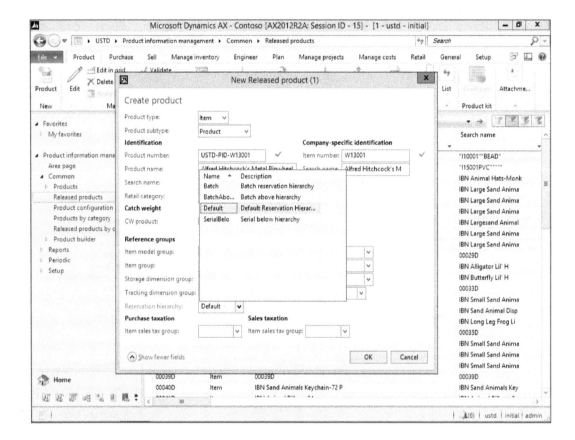

And then select the **Reservation Hierarchy.**

Creating A Warehouse Management Enabled Product

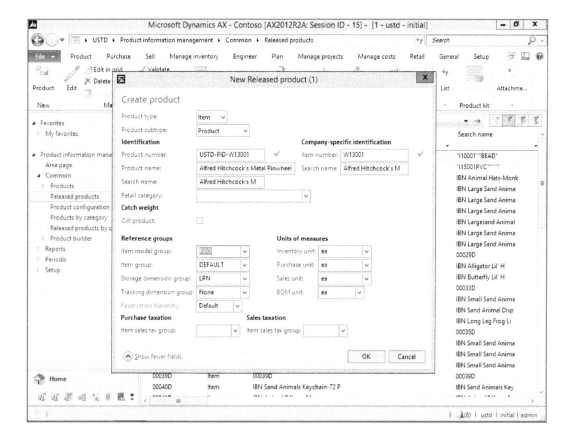

Finally, configure all of the default units of measure for the product.

After you have done that, just click on the **OK** button.

Creating A Warehouse Management Enabled Product

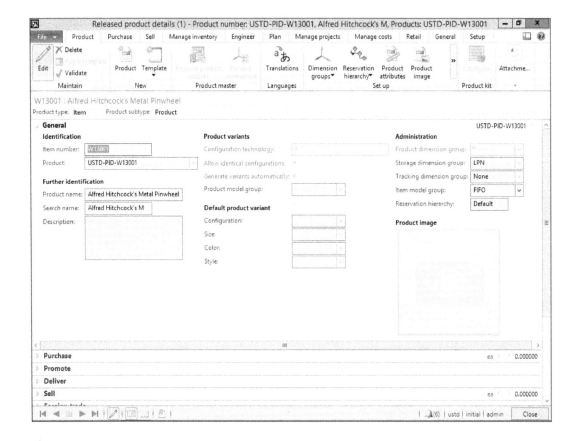

This will take you directly to the new **Released Product Details** form.

Creating A Warehouse Management Enabled Product

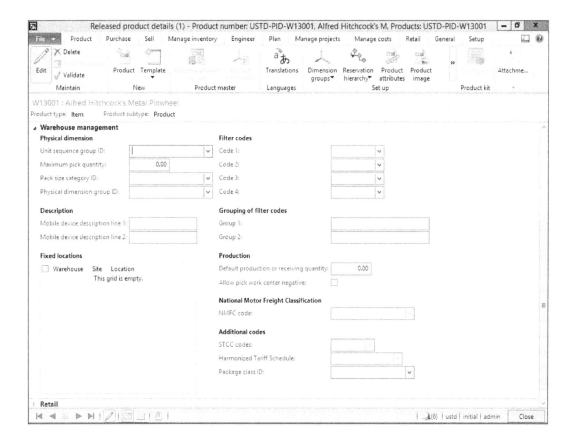

There is still a little bit more that we need to configure on the product though. So expand out the **Warehouse Management** tab group.

Creating A Warehouse Management Enabled Product

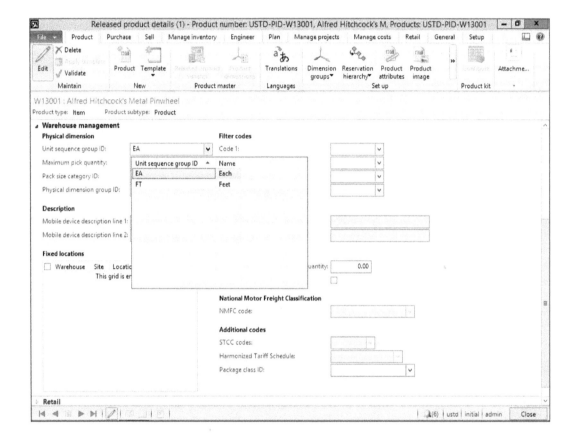

Click on the **Unit Sequence Group ID** dropdown and select the unit sequence group that matches the primary inventory unit for the product.

Creating A Warehouse Management Enabled Product

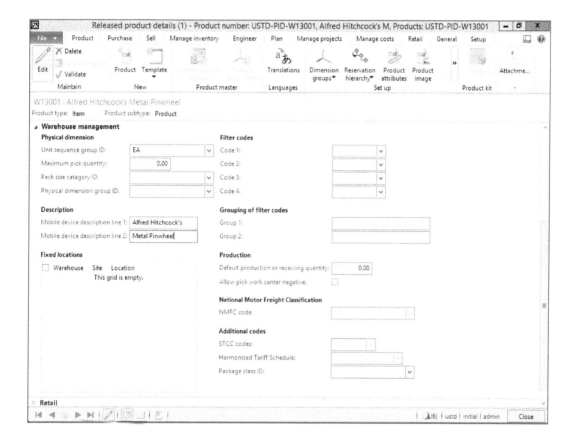

If you like, you can also override the default description that shows up on the handheld by setting the **Mobile Device Description Line 1** and **2** fields.

After you have done that your product is configured and you can exit from the form by clicking on the **Close** button.

CONFIGURING WORK

Next we need to configure how work is performed within the Warehouse Management system, and that entails configuring the rules as to how the picking, packing, and putaways are performed within the system and also when special rules are used by the system to manage the warehouse. This is also where you can make the system very elaborate, or reasonably simple. In the following examples we will err on the side of simplicity.

Setting Up Location Directives

The first step that we will work on is the configuration of the **Location Directives**. These are really just telling the system where do I want to pick product from, and where do I want to put it, and you will want to configure these for all of the main transactions like the Sales Order and the Purchase Order.

Setting Up Location Directives

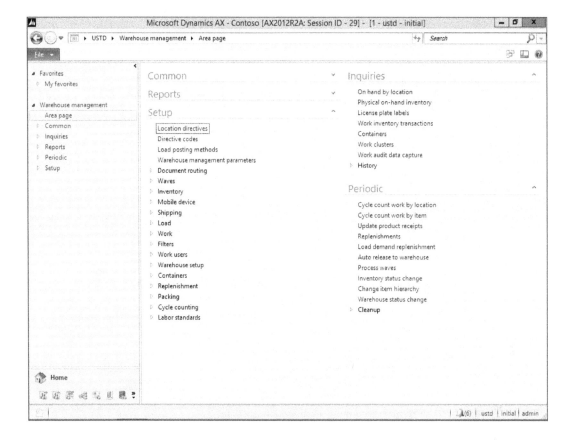

To do this, click on the **Location Directives** menu item within the **Setup** group of the **Warehouse Management** area page.

Setting Up Location Directives

This will open up the **Location Directives** maintenance form.

Setting Up Location Directives

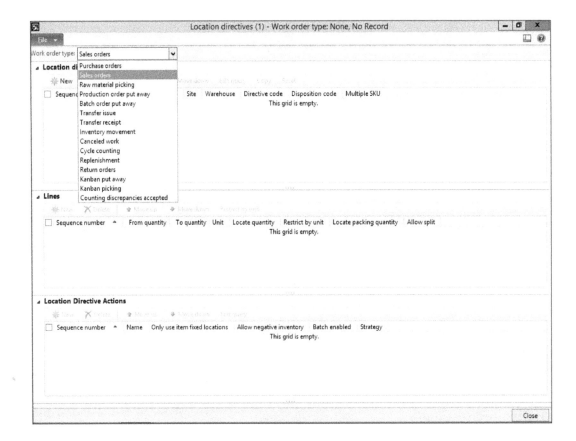

If you click on the **Work Order Type** dropdown list, you will see all of the different transactions that you can create work for. Start off though by setting it to the **Sales Order**.

Setting Up Location Directives

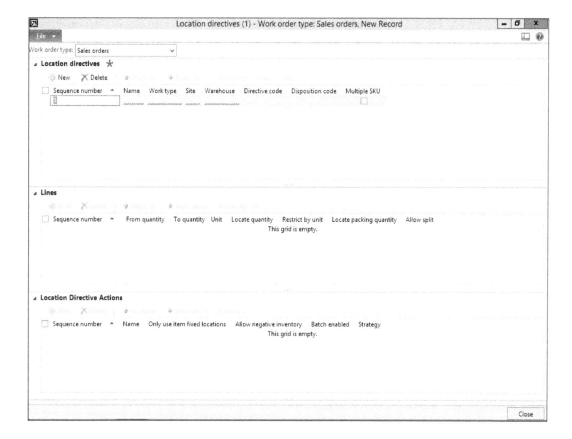

Within the first grid form for the **Location Directives**, click on the **New** button to create a new record.

Setting Up Location Directives

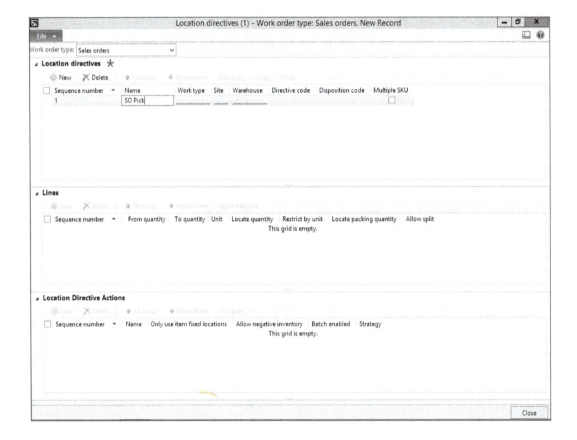

Set the **Sequence Number** to **1** and the **Name** to **SO Pick**.

Setting Up Location Directives

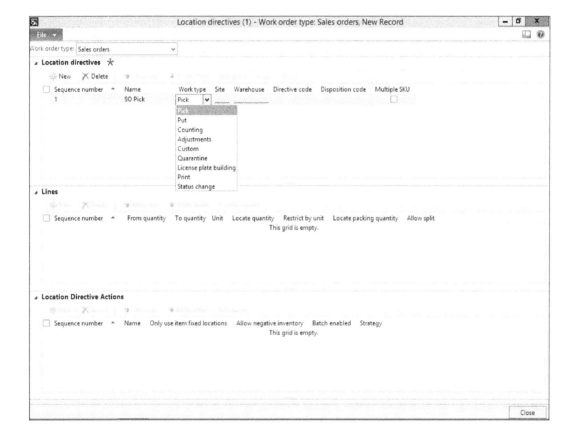

Click on the **Work Order** Dropdown list and select the **Pick** option to define the work for the sales order pick.

Setting Up Location Directives

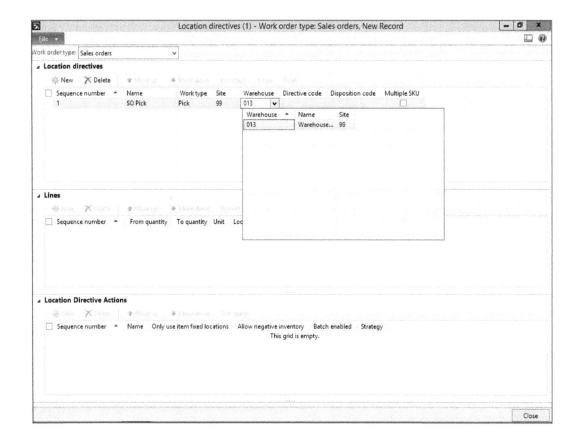

Then select the **Site** and the **Warehouse** that you want to configure the pick process for.

Setting Up Location Directives

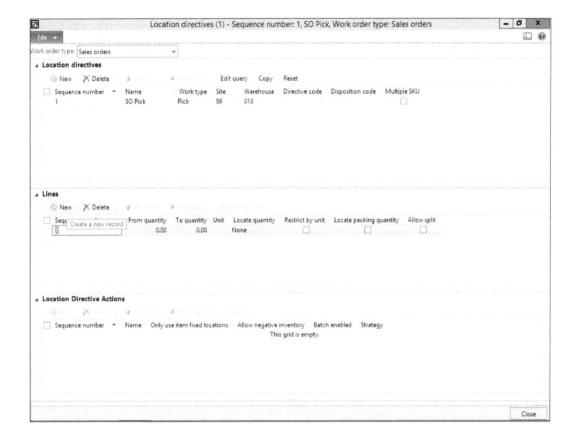

Then click on the **New** button within the **Lines** tab group to create a new record.

Setting Up Location Directives

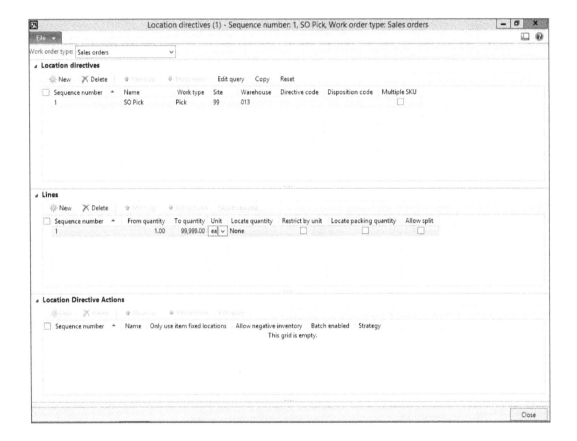

Set the **Sequence** to **1** and the **From** and **To Quantity** to a range that you want to set the work instructions for. This feature allows you to have different work instructions for different quantities.

Then set the **Unit** that you want to filter the work on. This allows you to have different instructions for different units – i.e. eachs and pallets.

Setting Up Location Directives

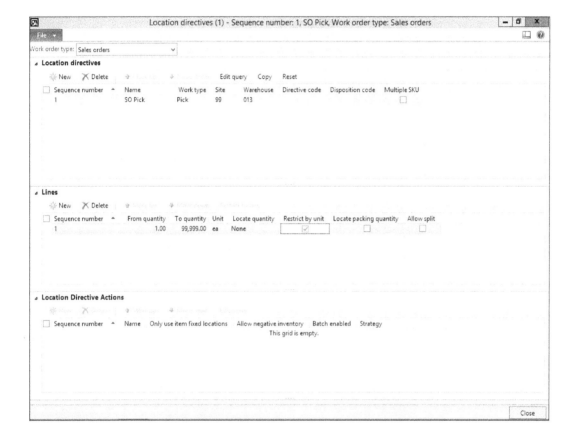

Then check the **Restrict By Unit** flag to indicate that you only want to use this instruction for that Unit Of Measure.

Setting Up Location Directives

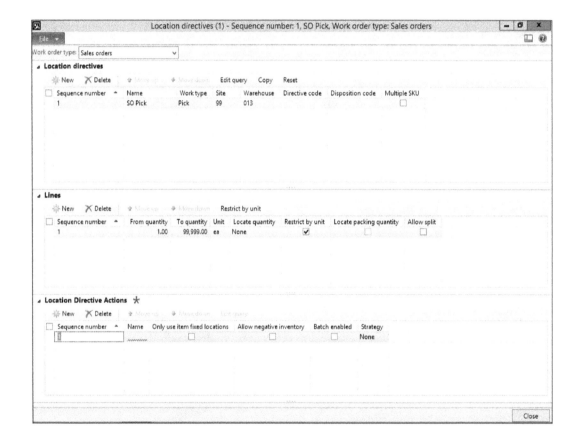

Now click on the **New** button within the **Location Directive Actions** to create a new action record for the Pick process.

Setting Up Location Directives

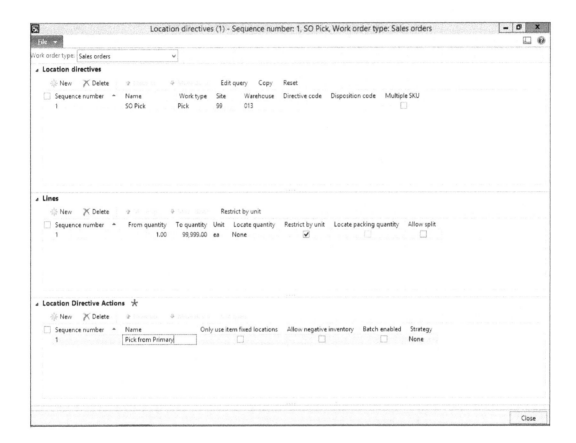

Set the **Sequence Number** to **1** and the **Name** to **Pick from Putaway**.

Setting Up Location Directives

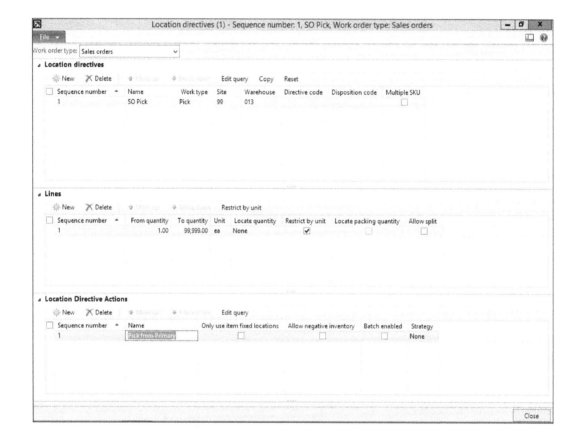

When you save the record, the **Edit Query** button will be enabled and you will be able to click on it.

Setting Up Location Directives

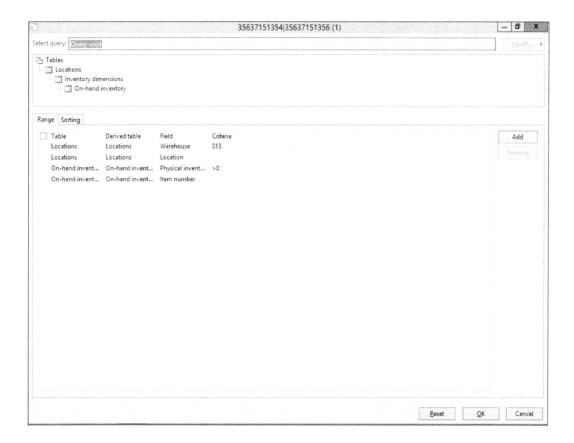

This will open up a new **Query Editor**.

Setting Up Location Directives

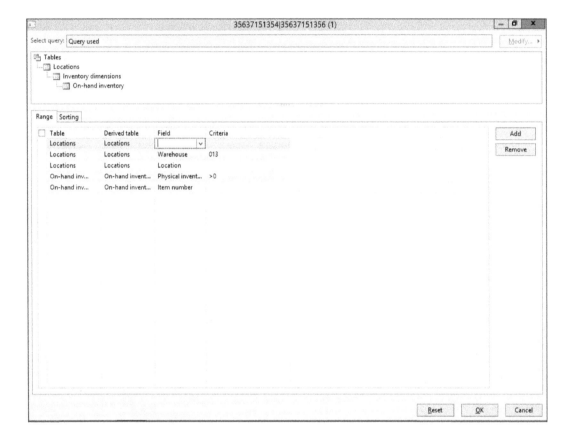

Click on the **Add** button to create a new line.

Setting Up Location Directives

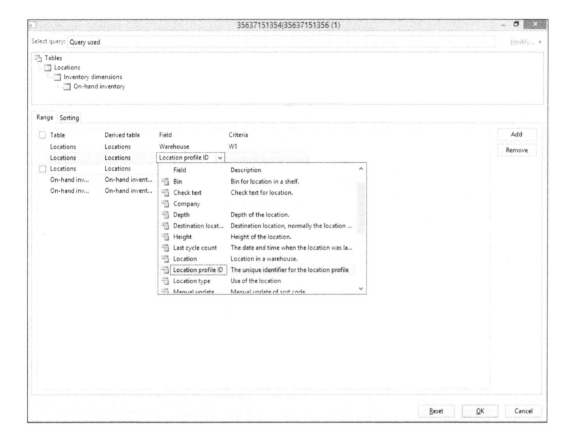

From the **Field** Dropdown, select the **Location Profile ID** field.

Setting Up Location Directives

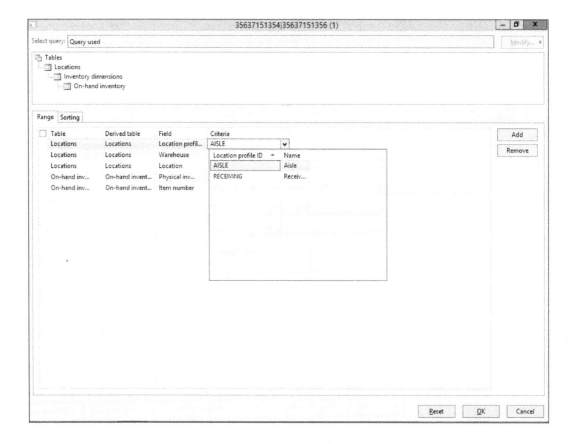

Then within the **Criteria** set the **Location Profile ID** to be **AISLE**.

Setting Up Location Directives

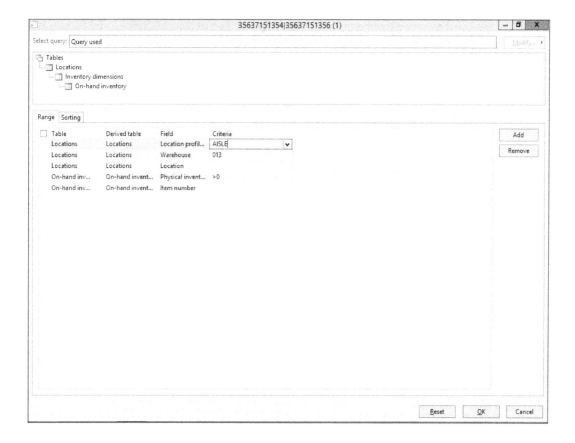

This is telling the system that it should pick a product from the Aisle locations only.

After you are done, just click on the **OK** button to save the query.

Setting Up Location Directives

Repeat the process again by adding another **Sales Order Location Directive**, and set the **Name** to **SO Put**, the **Work Type** to **Put** and the **Location Directive Action Name** to be **Put To Staging.**

Setting Up Location Directives

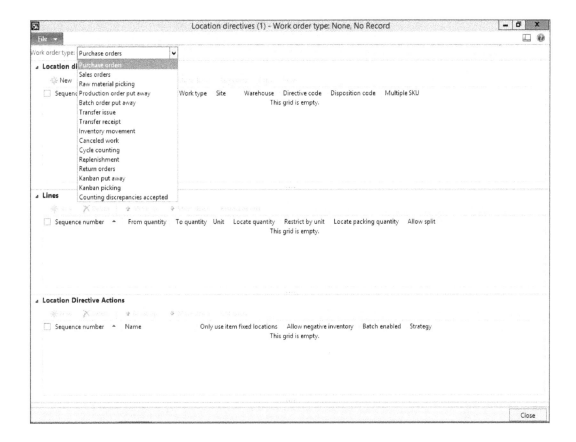

Then change the **Work Order Type** to **Purchase Orders**,

Setting Up Location Directives

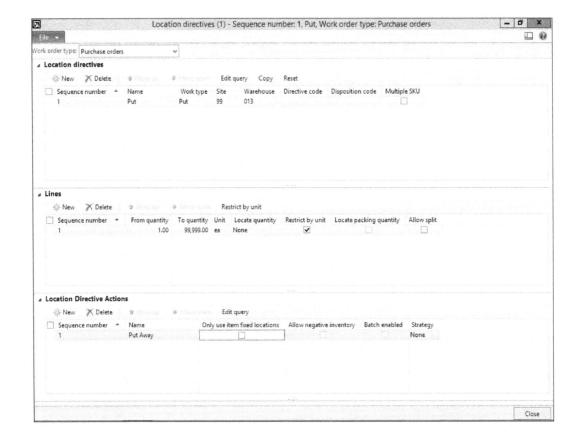

Create a new **Location Directive** for the **Purchase Order**, and set the **Name** to **Put**, the **Work Type** to **Put** and the **Location Directive Action Name** to be **Put Away.**

After you have done that, click on the **Close** button to exit from the form.

Configuring Wave Process Methods

Once we have our Location Directives configured, we can create our Wave Processes, but before we do that we just need to configure the **Wave Process Methods**.

Configuring Wave Process Methods

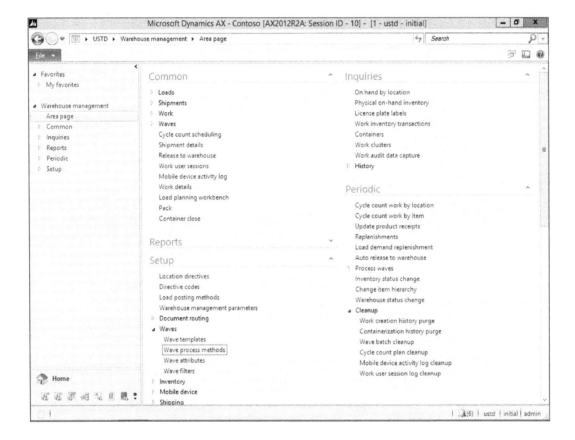

To do this, click on the **Wave Process Methods** menu item within the **Waves** folder of the **Setup** group within the **Warehouse Management** area page.

Configuring Wave Process Methods

When the **Wave Process Methods** maintenance form is displayed, click on the **Regenerate Methods** button in the menu bar.

Configuring Wave Process Methods

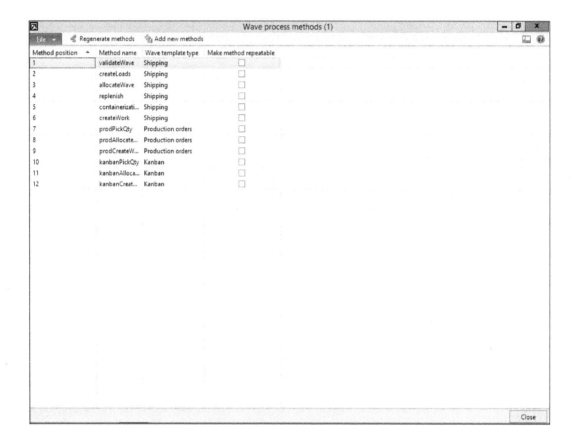

That will automatically create all of the methods that you need and you can click on the **Close** button to exit from the form.

Configuring A Wave Template

The next task is to configure a **Wave Template**. These define how a piece of work is to be done, and also the steps that are involved in the wave process.

Configuring A Wave Template

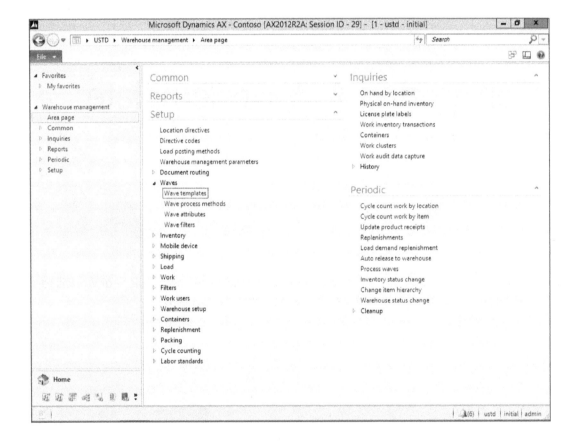

To do this, click on the **Wave Templates** menu item within the **Waves** folder of the **Setup** group within the **Warehouse Management** area page.

Configuring A Wave Template

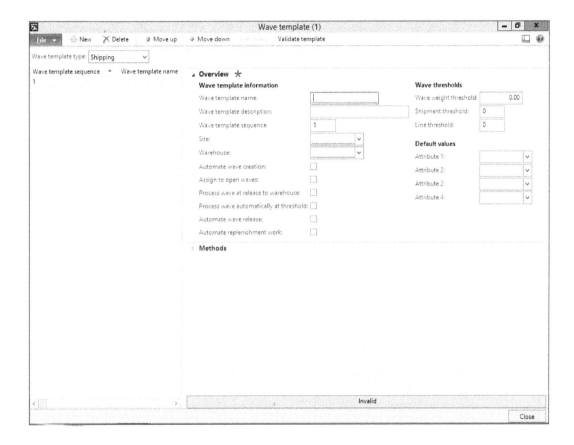

When the **Wave Template** maintenance form is displayed, set the **Wave Template Type** to **Staging** and then click on the **New** button in the menu bar to create a new record.

Configuring A Wave Template

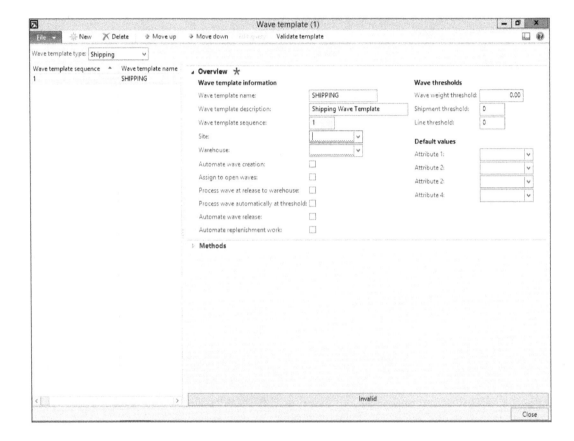

Set the **Wave Template** code to **SHIPPING** and the **Wave Template Description** to **Shipping Wave Template**.

Configuring A Wave Template

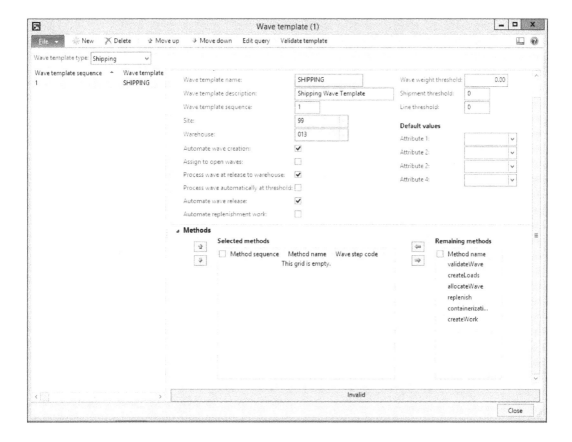

Then set the **Site** and **Warehouse** to be your WMS enabled site and warehouse.

Also check the **Automate Wave Creation**, **Process Wave At Release To Warehouse**, and **Automate Wave Release** flags.

Then expand out the **Methods** tab group.

Configuring A Wave Template

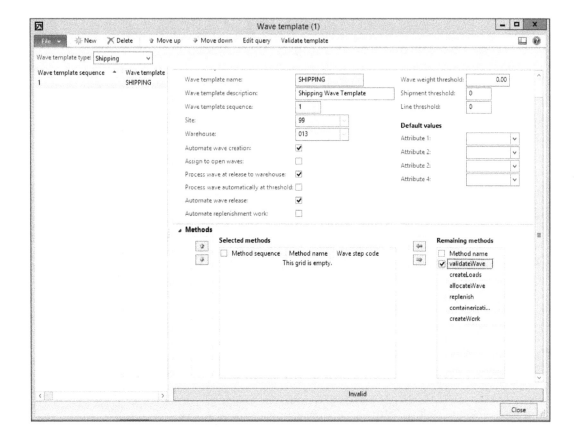

Within the **Remaining Methods** list, select the **validateWave** method and then click on the Left Arrow icon.

Configuring A Wave Template

This will move it to the **Selected Methods** list.

Configuring A Wave Template

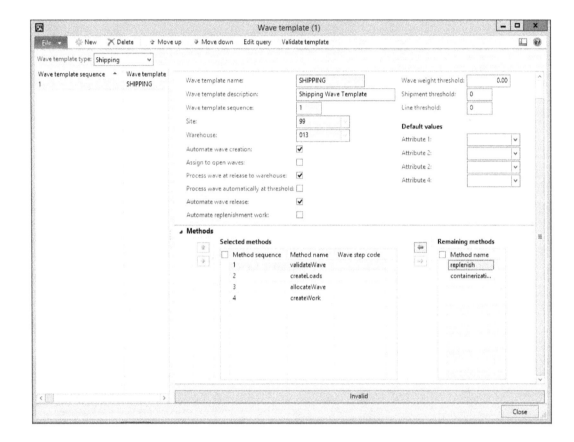

Repeat this process for the **createLoads**, **allocateWave**, and **CreateWork** methods.

Configuring A Wave Template

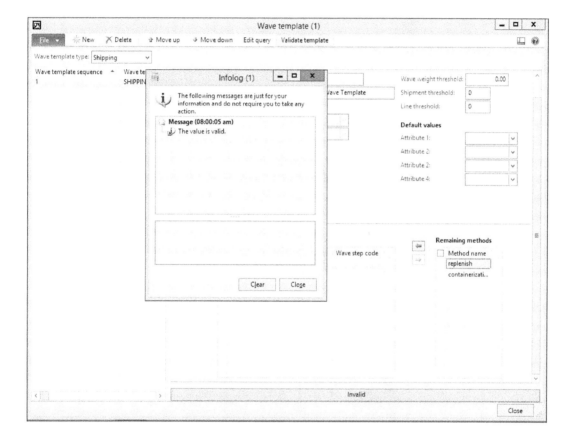

Now all that is left is to click the **Validate Template** button in the menu bar. If everything is set up correctly then you will get an InfoLog message saying that it validated.

Configuring A Wave Template

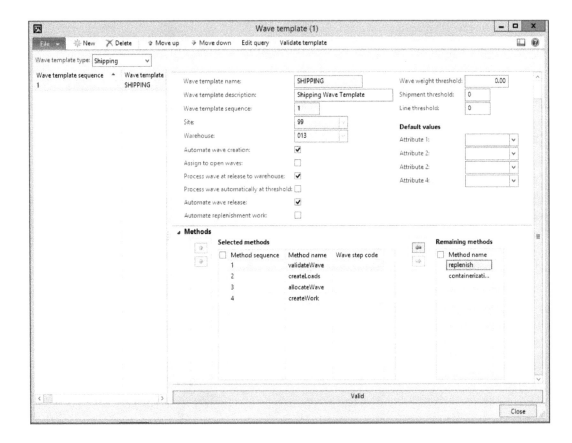

And your Wave Template will be marked as Valid in the footer.

Now you can click on the **Close** button and exit from the form.

Configuring Work Classes

Next we will define some **Work Classes** so that we can use them later on to classify the work that we will be ding by functional area.

Configuring Work Classes

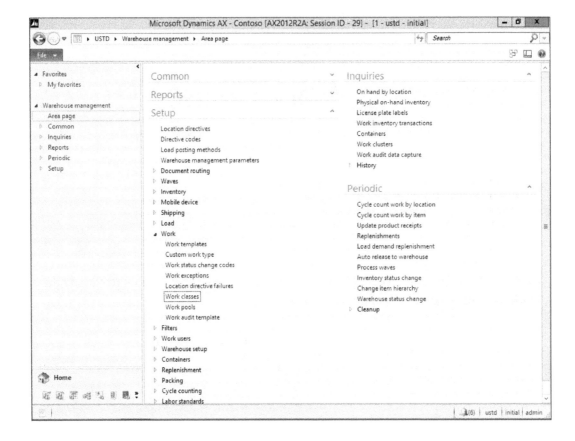

To do this, click on the **Work Classes** menu item within the **Work** folder of the **Setup** group within the **Warehouse Management** area page.

Configuring Work Classes

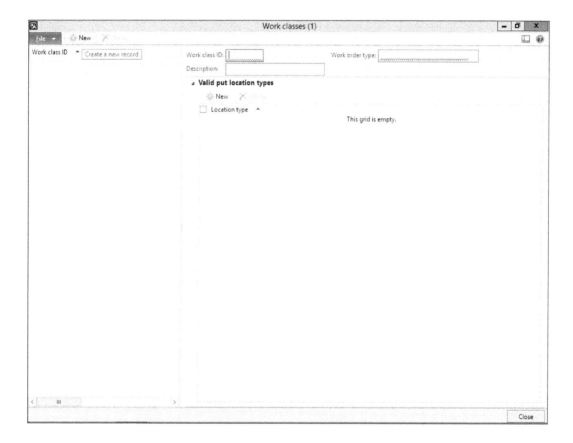

When the **Work Classes** maintenance form is displayed, click on the **New** button to create a new record.

Configuring Work Classes

Set the **Work Class ID** to **SALES** and the **Description** to **Sales**.

Configuring Work Classes

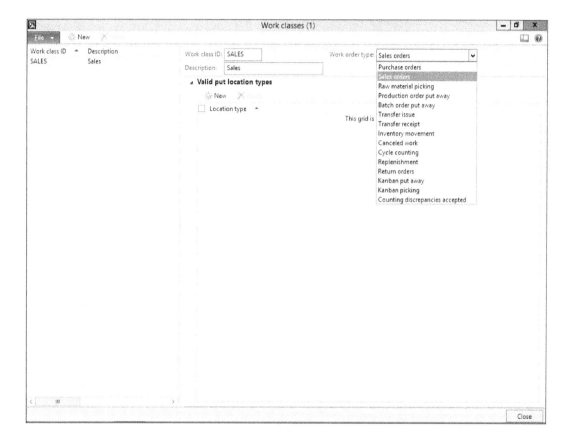

Then from the **Work Order Type**, select the **Sales Orders** value from the dropdown list.

Configuring Work Classes

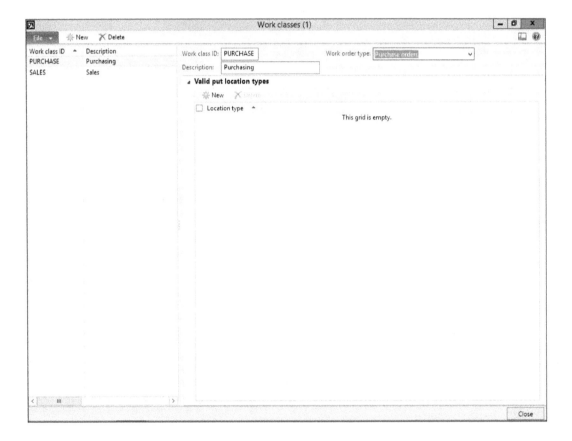

Click on the **New** button in the menu bar again to create another record, and set the **Work Class ID** to **PURCHASE**, the **Description** to **Purchasing** and the **Work Order Type** to **Purchase Order**.

After you have done that, just click on the **Close** button to exit from the form.

Configuring Work Templates

The final task that we need to do in this section is to configure some **Work Templates** that we will use to direct the workers.

Configuring Work Templates

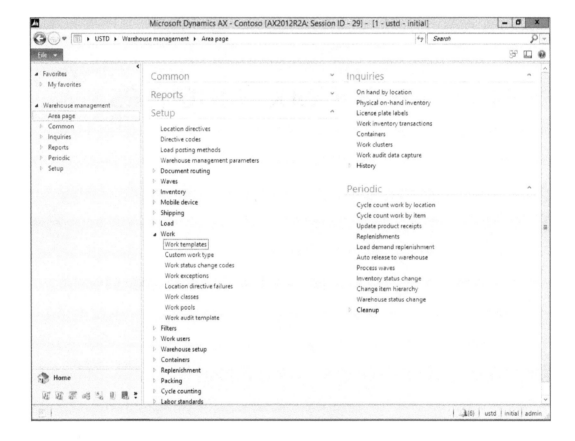

To do this, click on the **Work Templates** menu item within the **Work** folder of the **Setup** group within the **Warehouse Management** area page.

Configuring Work Templates

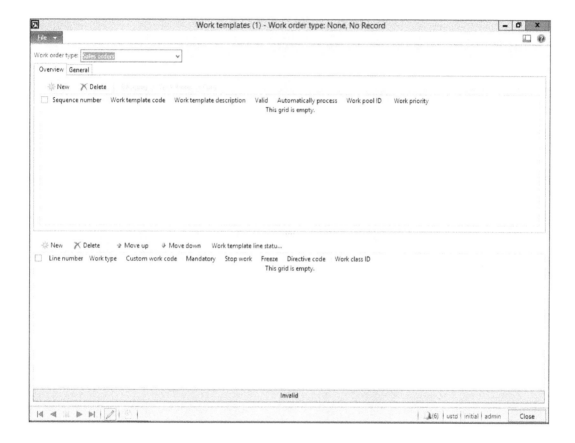

When the **Work Order Templates** maintenance form is displayed click on the **Work Order Type** field and select the **Sales Order** value.

Configuring Work Templates

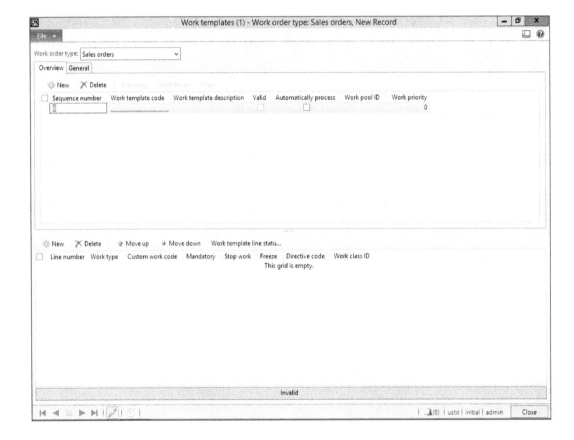

Then click on the **New** button within the **Overview** tab to create a new template.

Configuring Work Templates

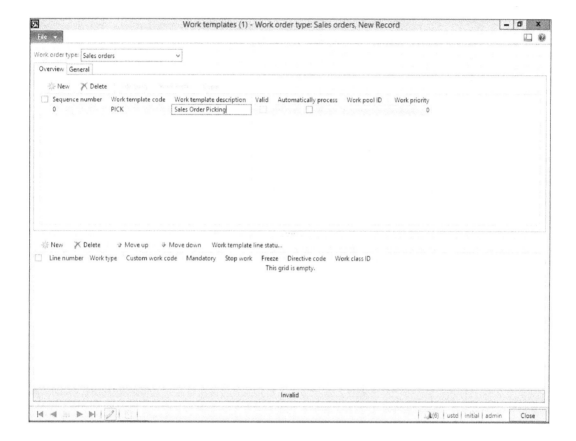

Set the **Work Template Code** to be **PICK** and the **Work Template Description** to be **Sales Order Picking**.

Configuring Work Templates

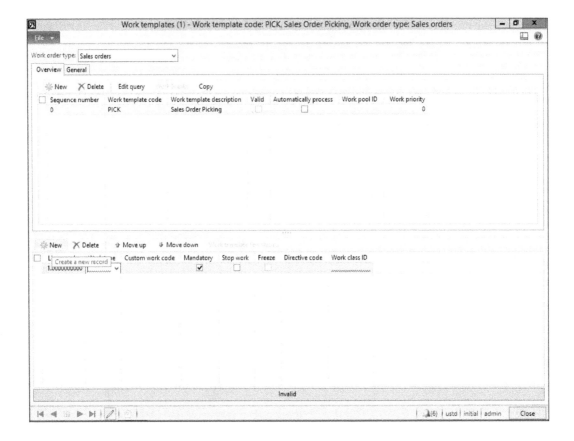

Within the footer grid for the template code, click on the **New** button to create a new work step.

Configuring Work Templates

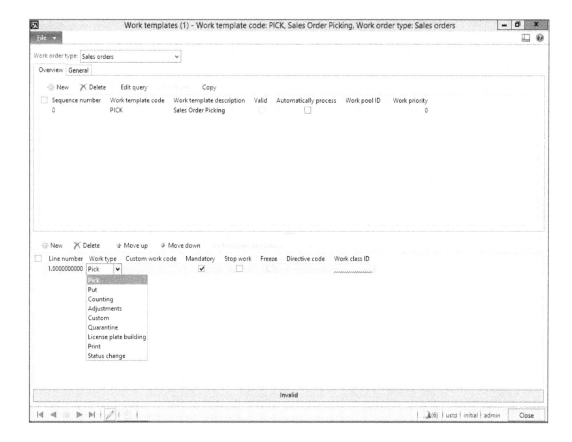

For the first line, click on the **Work Type** field and select the **Pick** record.

Configuring Work Templates

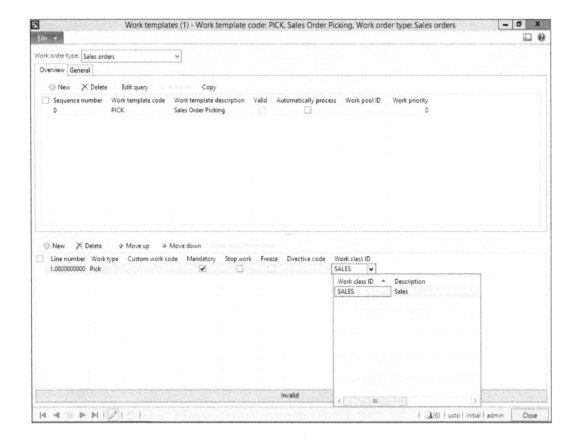

Then set the **Work Class ID** for the record to **SALES**.

Configuring Work Templates

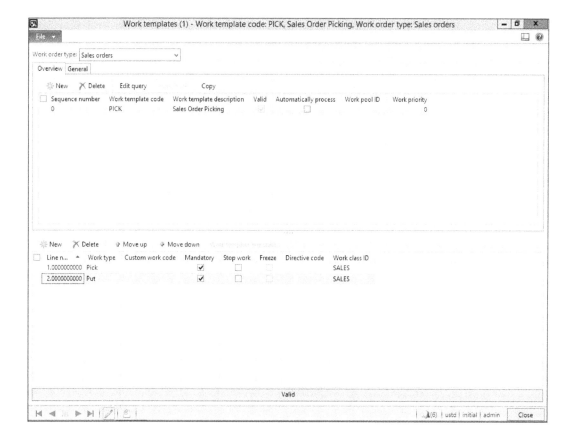

Click on the **New** button again to create a second work step, and set the **Work Type** to **Put** and the **Work Class ID** to **SALES**.

Configuring Work Templates

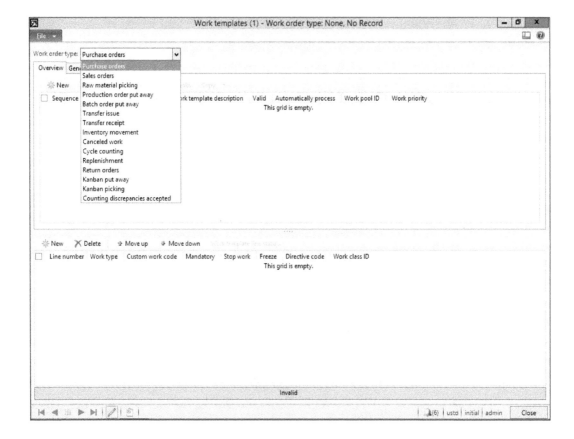

Now that we have the sales work template created we can create a template for purchasing. To do that, click on the **Work Order Type** dropdown list and select the **Purchase Orders** value.

Configuring Work Templates

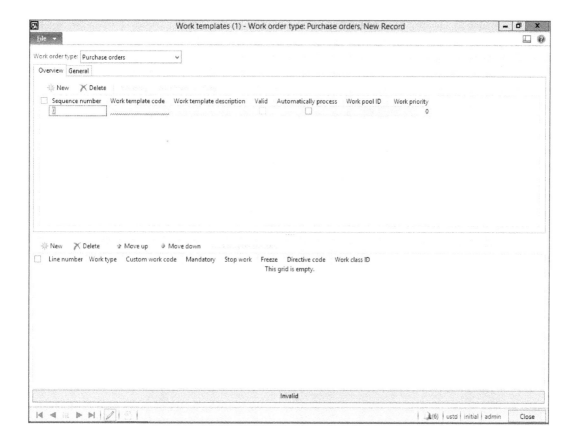

Then click on the **New** button within the **Overview** tab to create a new work template.

Configuring Work Templates

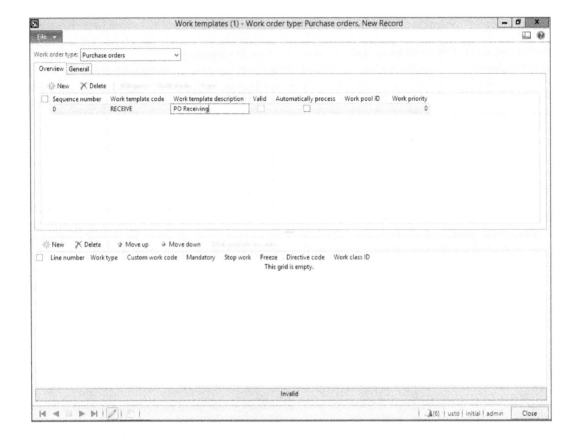

Set the **Work Template Code** to **RECEIVE** and the **Work Template Description** to **PO Receiving**.

Configuring Work Templates

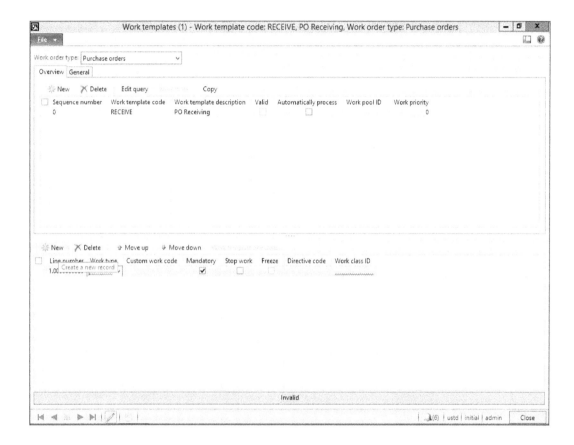

Within the footer grid for the template code, click on the **New** button to create a new work step.

Configuring Work Templates

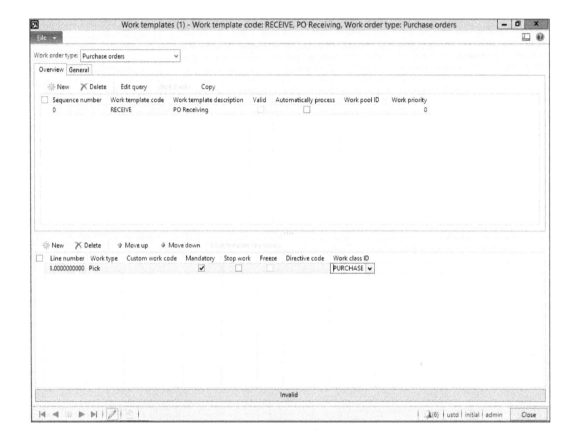

Set the **Work Type** to **Pick** and the **Work Class ID** to **PURCHASE**.

Configuring Work Templates

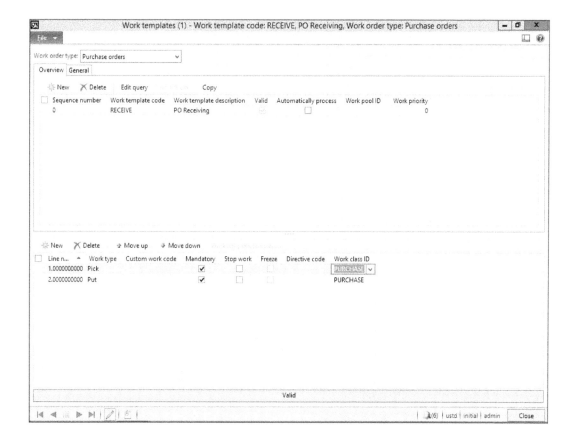

Click on the **New** button again to create a second work step, and set the **Work Type** to **Put** and the **Work Class ID** to **PURCHASE**.

Now we have all of our work configured, and we can click on the **Close** button to exit from the form.

CONFIGURING THE WAREHOUSE MANAGEMENT HANDHELD

One of the main reasons why you will want to use the Warehouse Management module within Dynamics AX is probably because of the in-built interface that you can use on handhelds which allows you to become more mobile and perform all of your tasks in real time. The bonus with this feature is that you can configure them directly within Dynamics AX without having to write a single line of code. So the next step in the setup process is to configure the handheld screens.

Setting Default Company for Warehouse Management Client

Before we start though there may be a little bit of housekeeping that we need to take care of. The handheld screens are linked to a default company that is associated with the user account that is administering the website. So if you want to use the handheld to access a new company then we need to point the handheld client to it.

Setting Default Company for Warehouse Management Client

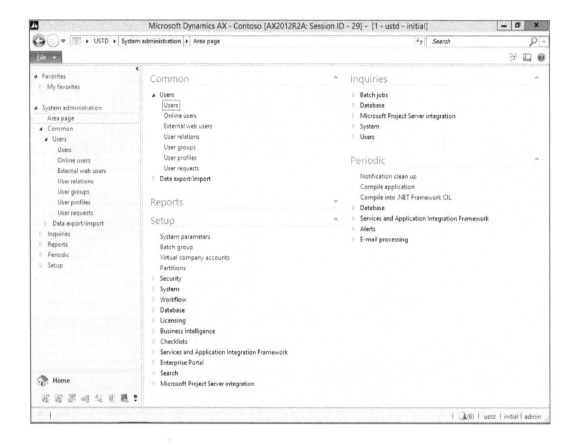

To do this click on the **Users** menu item within the **Users** folder of the **Common** group of the **System Administration** area page.

Setting Default Company for Warehouse Management Client

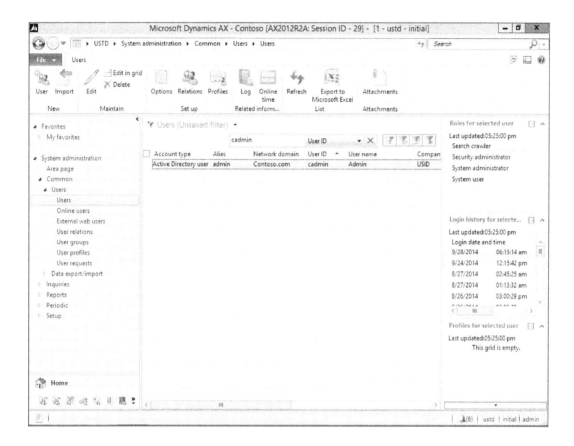

Filter out the users to the **cadmin** User ID. This is the default user that is associated with the handheld interface.

Setting Default Company for Warehouse Management Client

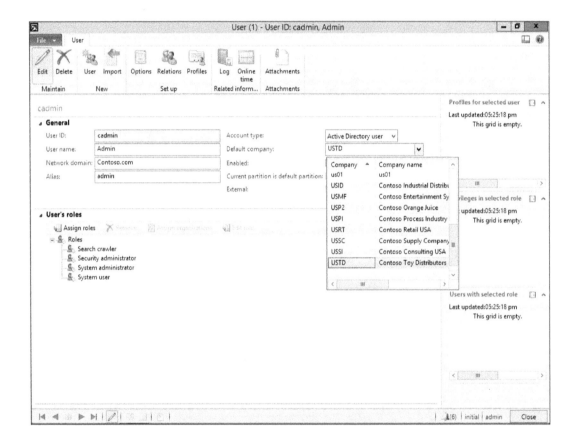

If you open up the users detail page then you can select the **Default Company** that you want to use when you use the handheld screens.

Setting Default Company for Warehouse Management Client

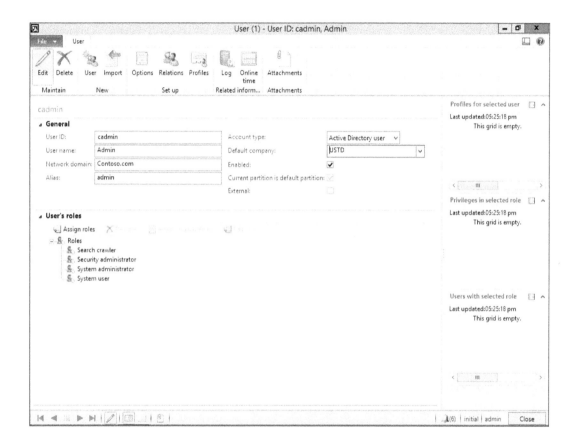

All you need to do is change it, save the record (**CTRL+S**) and then click the **Close** button to exit from the form.

Configuring Purchasing Menu Items

Now we can start building our menus that we will show on the handheld, and that entails configuring our menu items. We will start that process by creating the purchasing menu items.

Configuring Purchasing Menu Items

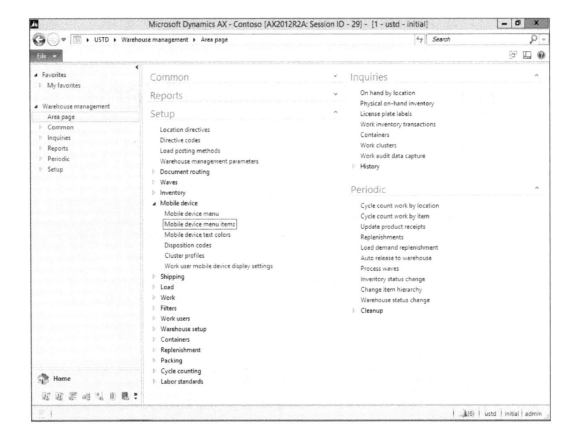

To do this, click on the **Mobile Device Menu Items** menu item within the **Mobile Device** folder of the **Setup** group within the **Warehouse Management** area page.

Configuring Purchasing Menu Items

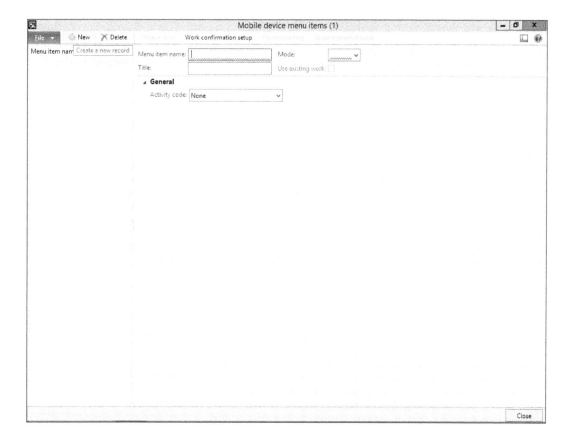

When the **Mobile Device Menu Items** maintenance form is displayed, click on the **New** button in the menu bar to create a new record.

Configuring Purchasing Menu Items

Set the **Menu Item Name** to **PO Receipt** and the **Title** to **PO Receipt**.

Configuring Purchasing Menu Items

Set the **Mode** for the menu item to be **Work**.

Configuring Purchasing Menu Items

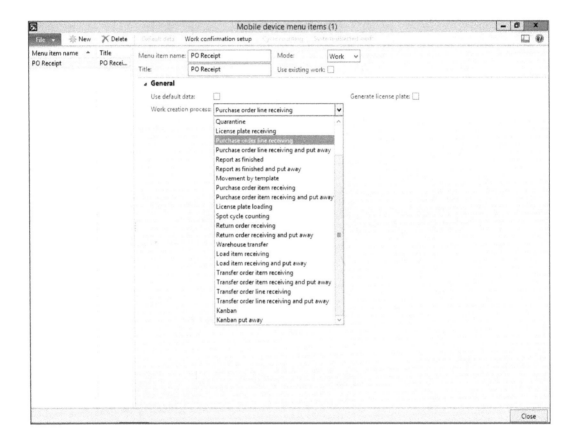

Then within the **General** tab group, click on the **Work Creation Type** field and select the **Purchase Order Line Receiving** value to tell the system to perform a receipt from this menu item.

Configuring Purchasing Menu Items

This will make a few more fields visible, and you will be able to check the **License Plate Grouping** field.

Configuring Purchasing Menu Items

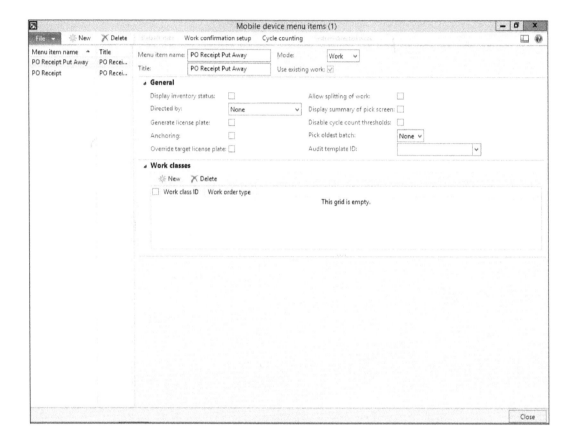

Click on the **New** button in the menu bar again to create a new record. For this record, set the **Menu Item Name**, and **Title** to be **PO Receipt Put Away**, set the **Mode** to **Work** and check the **Use Existing Work** flag.

Configuring Purchasing Menu Items

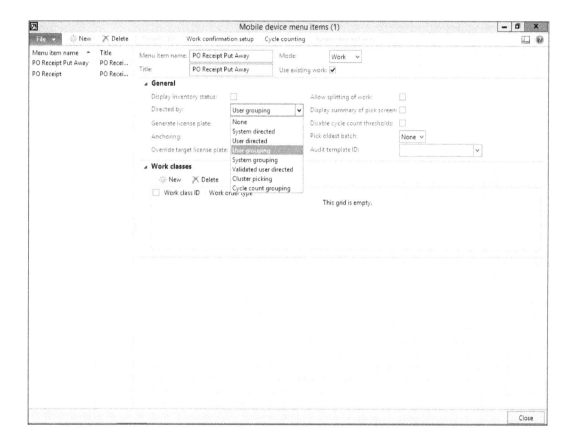

Click on the **Directed By** dropdown list and select the **User Grouping** option.

Configuring Purchasing Menu Items

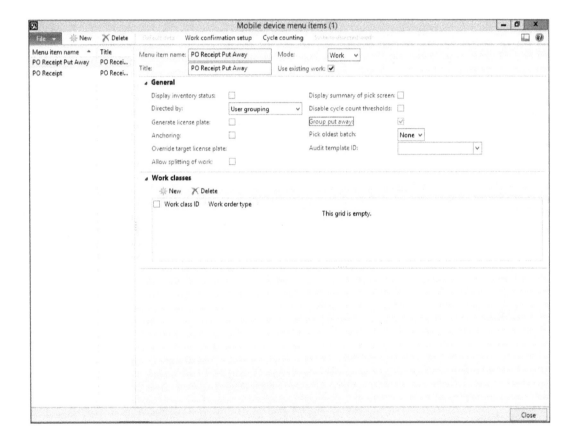

And then check the **Group Put Away** flag.

Configuring Purchasing Menu Items

Within the **Work Classes** grid, click on the **New** button to create a new record.

Configuring Purchasing Menu Items

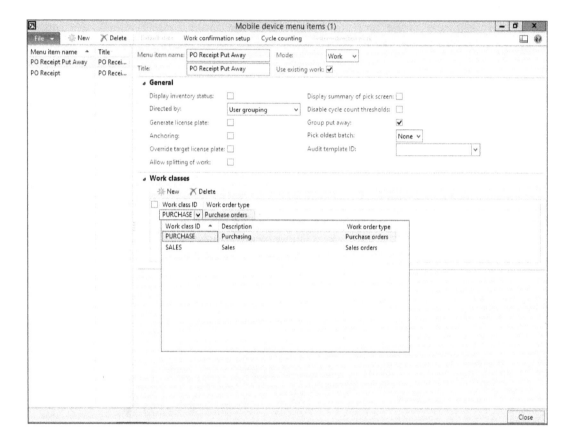

Click on the **Work Class ID** dropdown and select the **PURCHASE** record.

Configuring Purchasing Menu Items

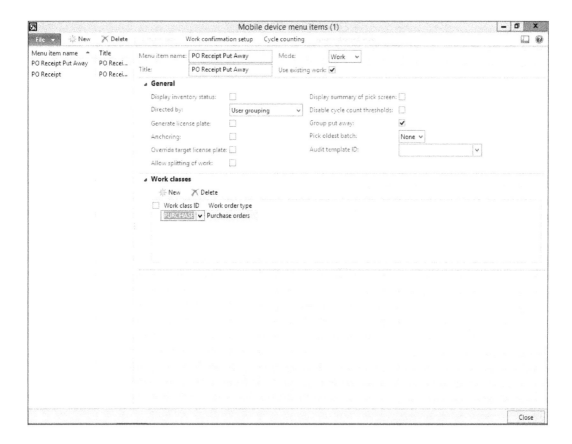

Now you have the menu items for purchasing configured.

Configuring Navigation Menu Items

Next we will set up the navigation menu items that you will want to have on your menus.

Configuring Navigation Menu Items

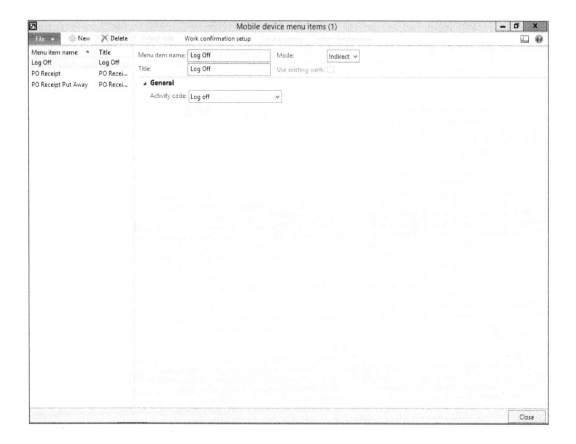

To do this, return to the **Mobile Device Menu Items** form, and click on the **New** button in the menu bar.

Set the **Menu Item Name** and **Title** to be **Log Off**, the **Mode** to **Indirect**, and the **Activity Code** to **Log Off.**

Configuring Sales Menu Items

The final set of menu items that we will configure will be the Sales functions.

Configuring Sales Menu Items

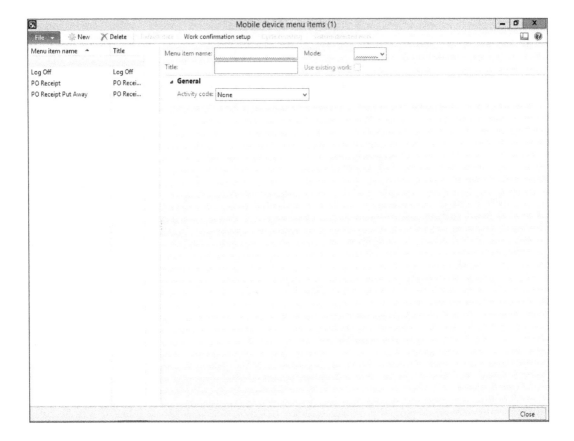

To do this, return to the **Mobile Device Menu Items** form, and click on the **New** button in the menu bar.

Configuring Sales Menu Items

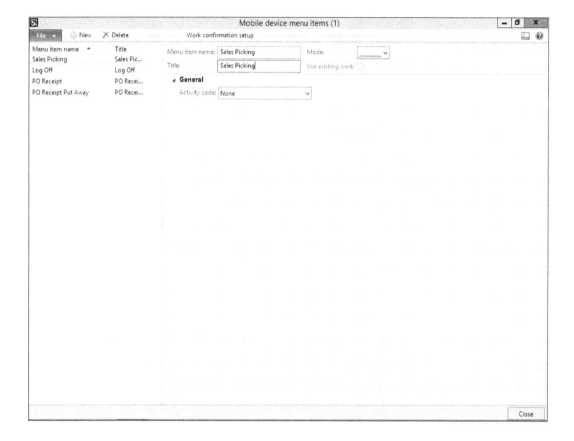

Set the **Menu Item Name** and **Title** to **Sales Picking**.

Configuring Sales Menu Items

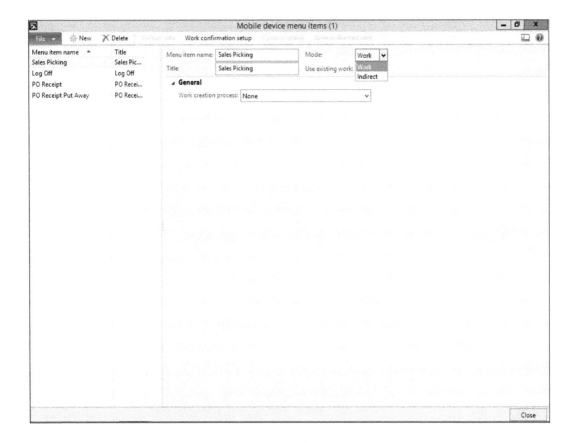

Set the **Mode** to be **Work**.

Configuring Sales Menu Items

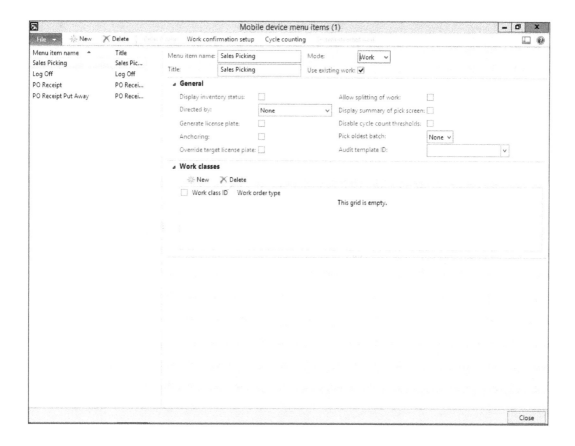

And then check the **Use Existing Work** flag on the record.

Configuring Sales Menu Items

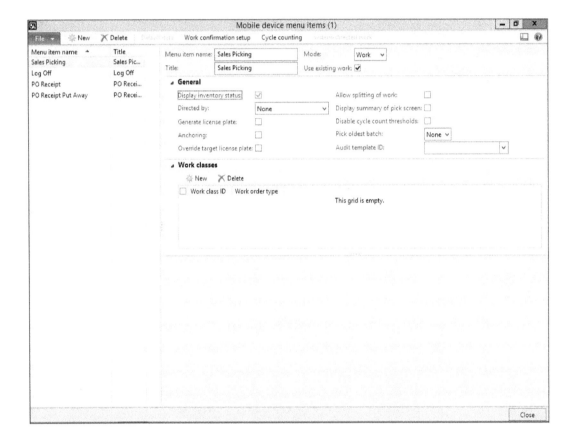

Within the **General** tab group, check the **Display Inventory Status** flag.

Configuring Sales Menu Items

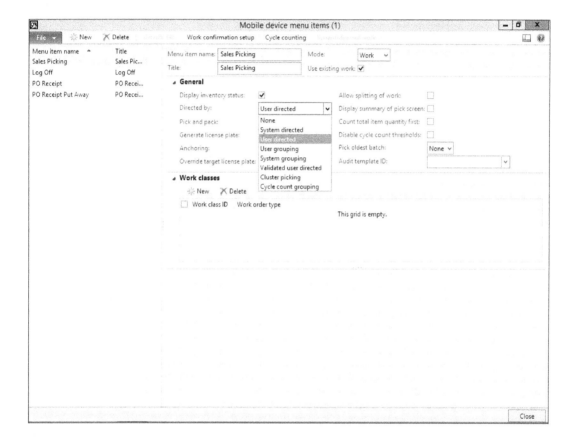

Click on the **Directed By** dropdown list and select the **User Directed** option.

Configuring Sales Menu Items

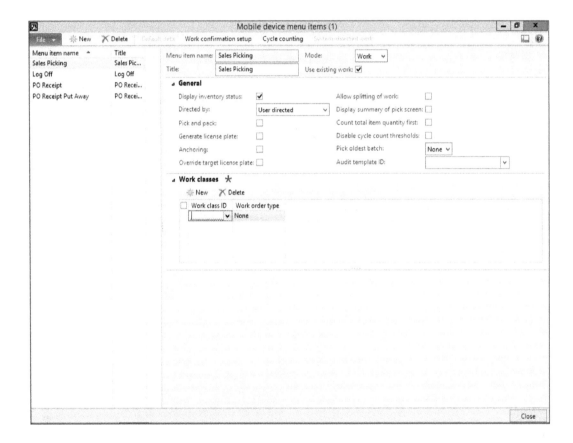

Within the **Work Classes** grid, click on the **New** button to create a new record.

Configuring Sales Menu Items

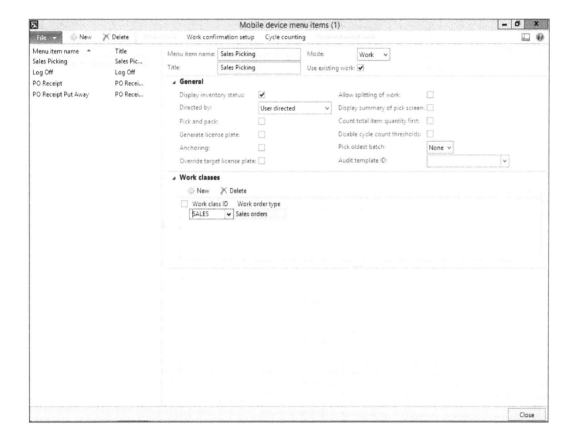

And set the **Work Class ID** to be **SALES**.

Configuring Sales Menu Items

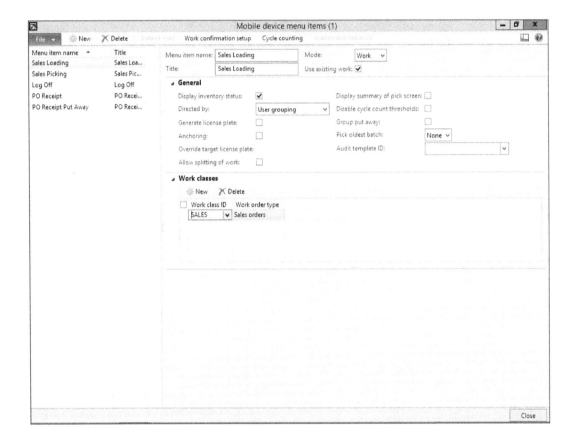

Click on the **New** button in the menu bar one more time to create a new record, and set the **Menu Item Name** and **Title** to **Sales Loading**. Set the **Mode** to **Work**, check the **Use Existing Work**, and **Display Inventory Status** flags, and set the **Directed By** field to **User Grouping**. Finally add a new **Work Class** and set it to **SALES**.

After you have done that you are done, and you can click on the **Close** button to exit from the form.

Configuring Menus

Now that we have our menu items, we can create our menus that we will show on the handheld.

Configuring Menus

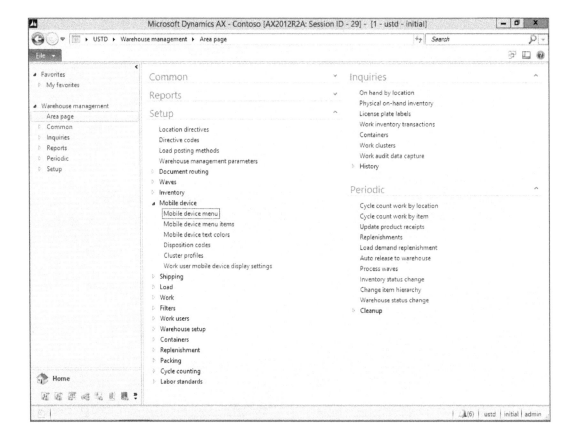

To do this, click on the **Mobile Device Menu** menu item within the **Mobile Device** folder of the **Setup** group within the **Warehouse Management** area page.

Configuring Menus

When the **Mobile Device Menus** maintenance form is displayed, click on the **New** button within the menu bar to create a new menu.

Configuring Menus

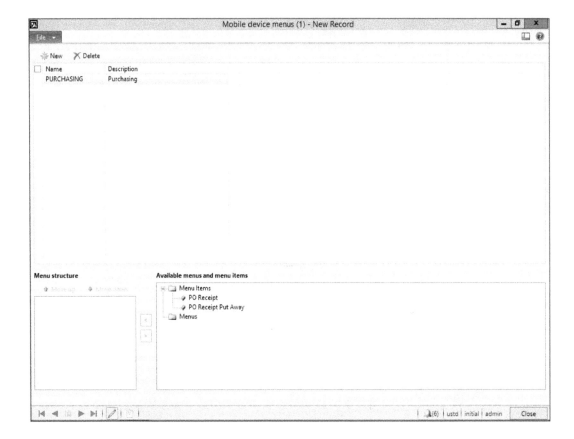

For the first menu, set the **Name** to be **PURCHASING** and the **Description** to **Purchasing.**

Configuring Menus

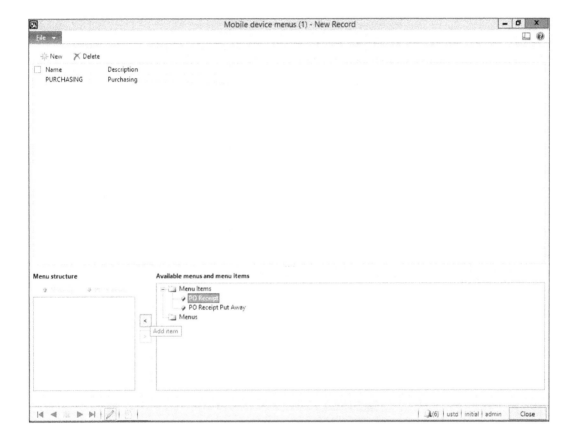

Within the **Available Menus And Menu Items** selector you will be able to see all of the menu items that you created. Select the **PO Receipt** menu item and then click on the < button to add it to the menu structure.

Configuring Menus

You will see that the menu is being built within the **Menu Structure** tree view.

Configuring Menus

Repeat the step and ass the **PO Receipt Put Away** menu item.

Configuring Menus

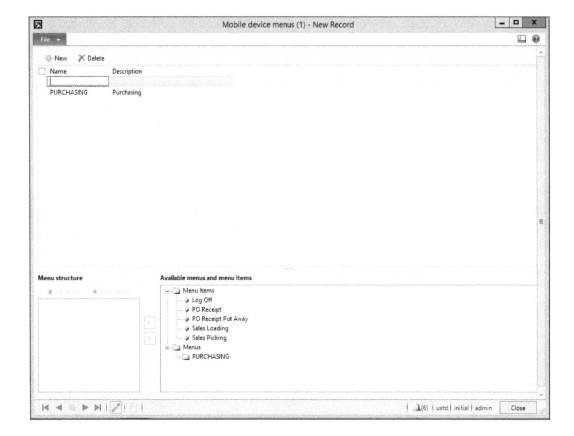

Now click on the **New** button in the menu bar again so that we can create a new sub-menu for our sales tasks.

Configuring Menus

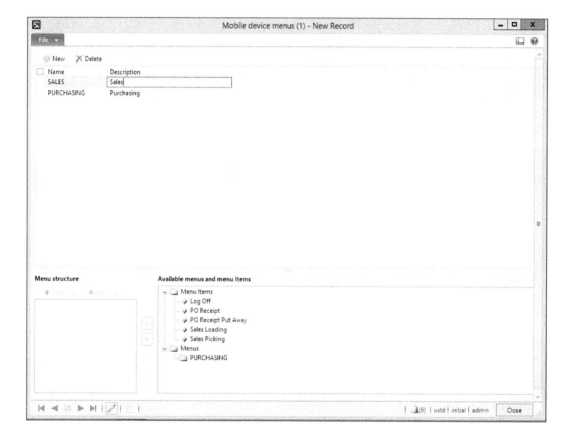

Set the **Name** to be **SALES** and the **Description** to **Sales**.

Configuring Menus

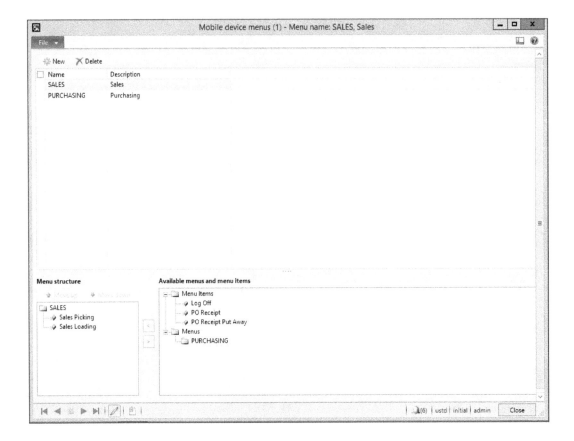

For this menu, add the **Sales Picking** and **Sales Loading** menu items.

Configuring Menus

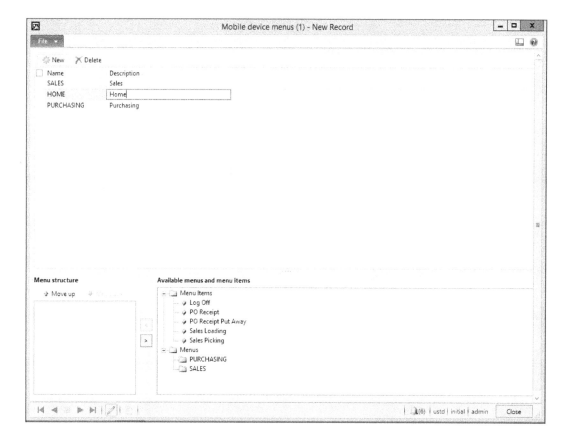

Click on the **New** button in the menu bar one last time to create a parent menu to hold our sub-menus. Set the **Name** to be **HOME** and the **Description** to be **Home**.

Configuring Menus

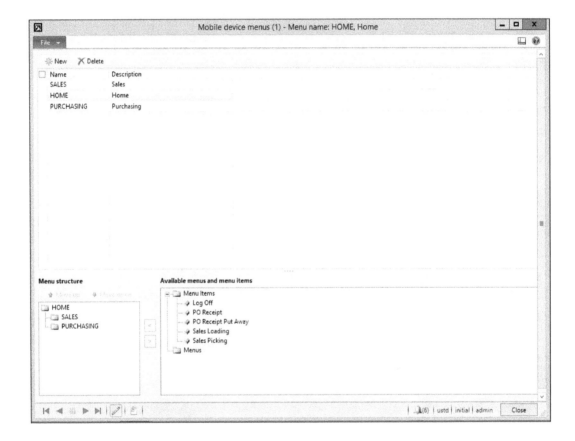

For this menu structure add the **SALES** and **PURCHASING** menus.

Configuring Menus

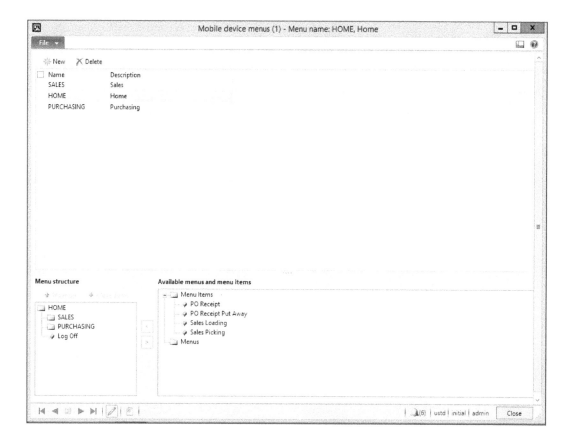

Then click on the **Log Off** menu item, and add it to the end of the menu structure.

Now that you have configured your initial menu, click on the **Close** button to exit from the form.

Configuring Mobile Display Settings

The final step in the setup of the mobile client is to tweak some of the display settings.

Configuring Mobile Display Settings

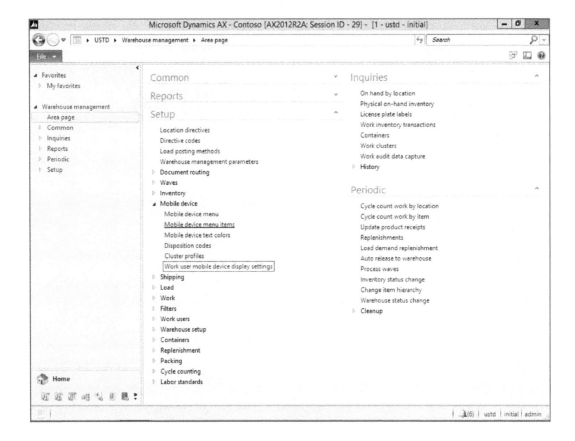

To do this click on the **Work User Mobile Device Display Settings** menu item within the **Mobile Device** folder of the **Setup** group within the **Warehouse Management** area page.

Configuring Mobile Display Settings

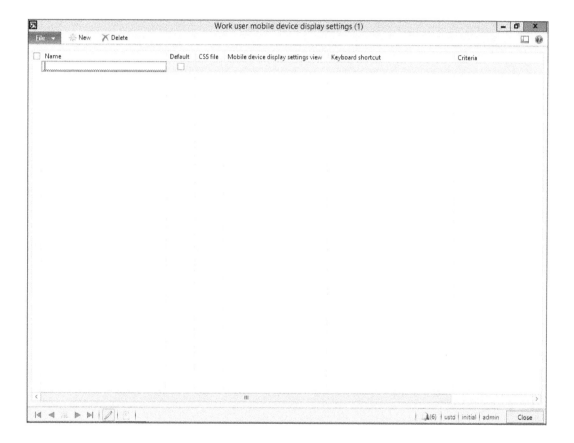

When the **Work User Mobile Device Settings** maintenance form is displayed, click on the **New** button to create a new record.

Configuring Mobile Display Settings

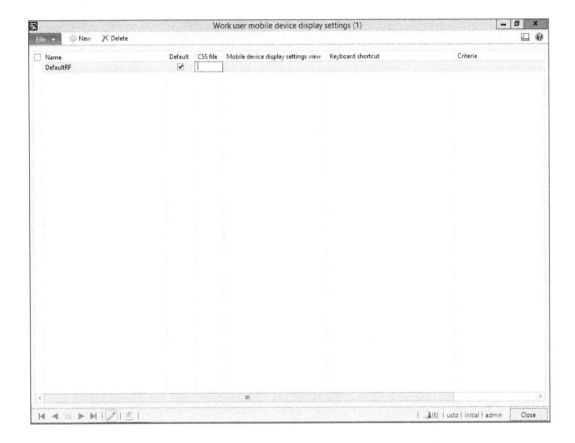

Set the **Name** to **DefaultRF** and also check the **Default** flag to say that you want to use this view by default.

Configuring Mobile Display Settings

Set the **CSS File** to **defaultrf.css**.

Configuring Mobile Display Settings

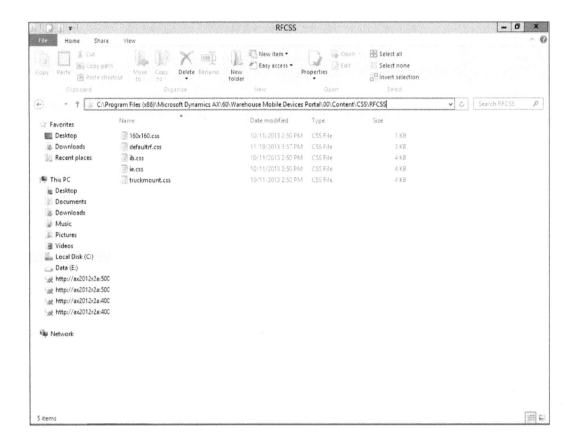

The .css file is the style sheet that tells the system how to format the handheld screen, and a tip that you may want to know is that if you look in the **Warehouse Mobile Deices Portal** folder, then you will see that there are a number of them available, including larger truck mount versions. This is also where you can design your own .css files.

Configuring Mobile Display Settings

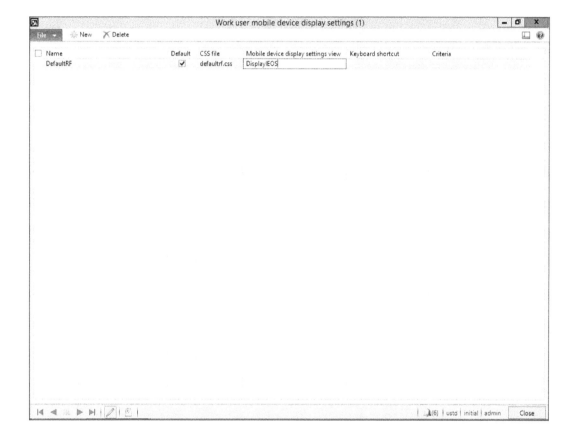

Finally, set the **Mobile Device Display Settings View** to **DisplayIEOS**.

Now you can click on the **Close** button and exit out of the form.

CONFIGURING WORKERS

The final piece of setup that is required is to set up your workers so that they can start doing the work.

Configuring Worker Logins

The only setup that is required is to set up the worker record within Warehouse Management and assign them to their warehouses.

Configuring Worker Logins

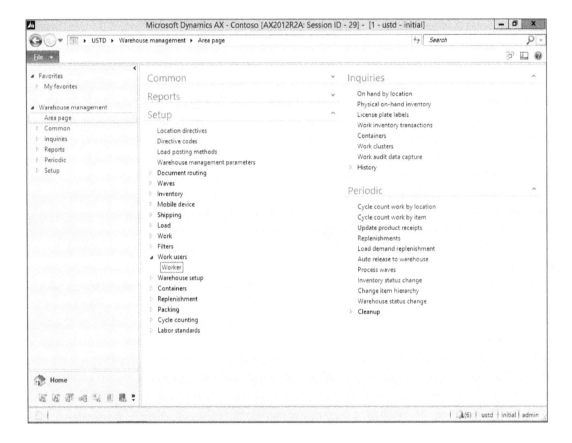

To do this click on the **Worker** menu item within the **Work Users** folder of the **Setup** group within the **Warehouse Management** area page.

Configuring Worker Logins

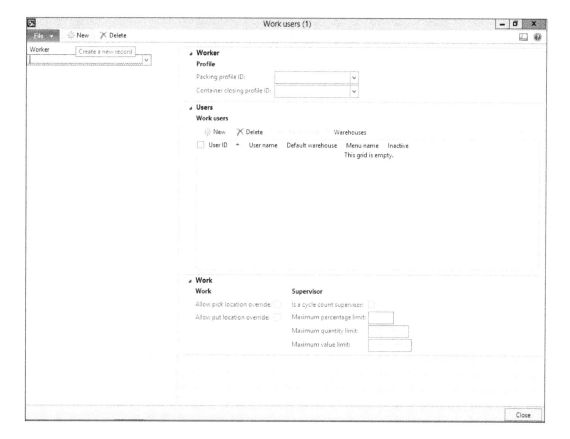

When the **Work Users** maintenance form is displayed, click on the **New** button in the menu bar to create a new record.

Configuring Worker Logins

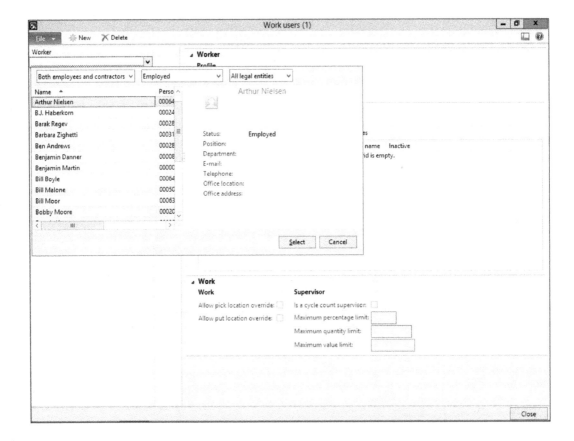

From the **Worker** dropdown list, select the employee that you want to configure to use the handheld devices.

Configuring Worker Logins

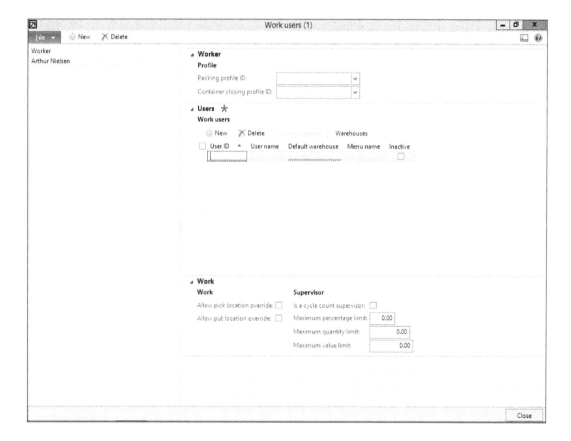

A worker may have multiple logins for multiple warehouses so we will need to set up the WMS login and credentials for them as well. To do this click on the **New** button within the **Work Users** tab group.

Configuring Worker Logins

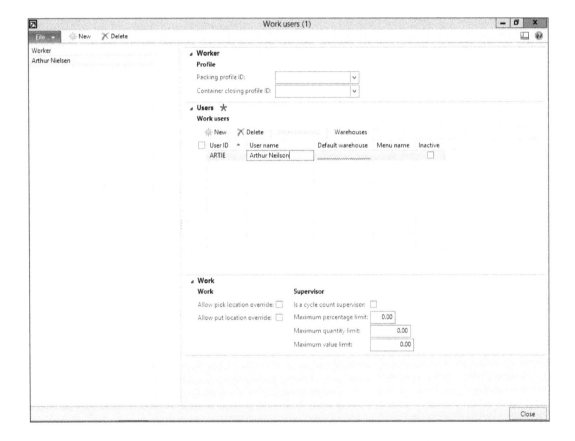

Give your **Work User** a **User ID** that they will use to log into the handhelds and also a **User Name**.

Configuring Worker Logins

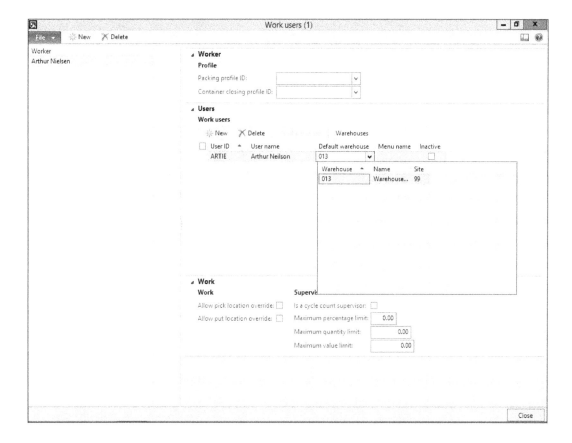

Then select the **Default Warehouse** from the dropdown list of WMS enabled warehouses.

Configuring Worker Logins

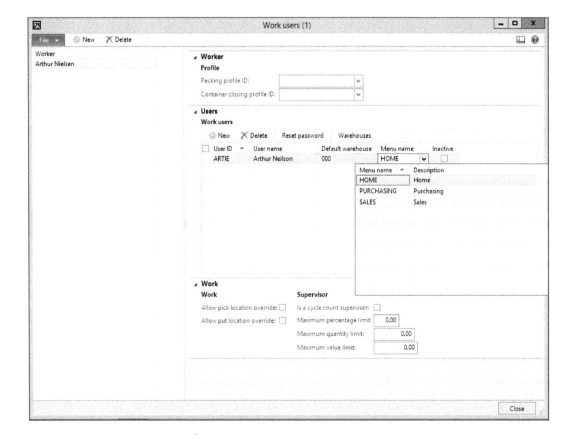

Then select the menu that you want the user to access by selecting it from the **Menu Name** drop down list.

Configuring Worker Logins

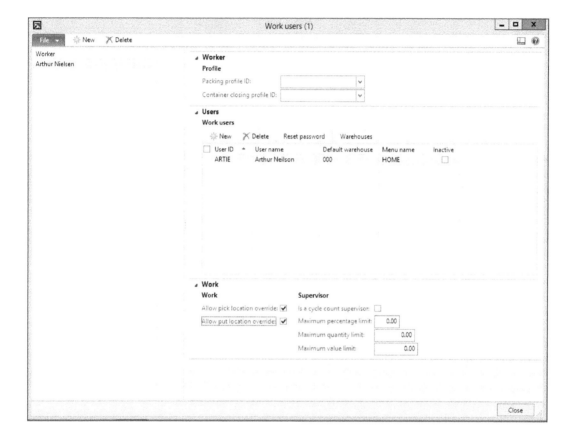

Then check the **Allow Pick Location Override** and **Allow Put Location Override** flags to give the user a little creative freedom.

Configuring Worker Logins

Finally we need to set the users password. To do this click on the **Reset Password** menu item within the **Work Users** menu bar.

Configuring Worker Logins

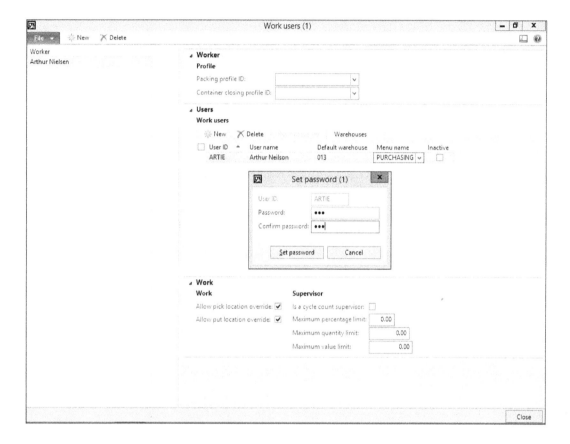

When the **Set Password** dialog box is displayed, enter in the password and then click on the **Set Password** button.

Configuring Worker Logins

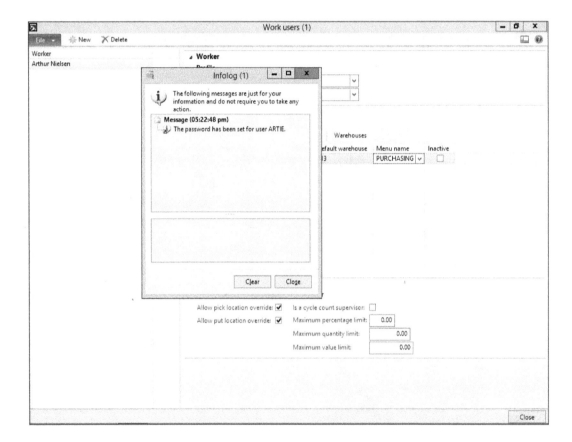

You will get a notification that the password was set and you can close out of the InfoLog.

Configuring Worker Logins

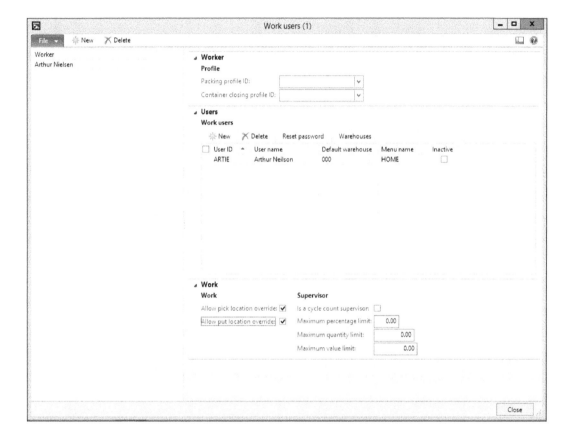

Now your user is configured. You can continue to add more users, and when you are done, just click on the **Close** button to exit from the form.

Accessing Data Collection

Now we have everything configured, we can test drive the Warehouse Management by logging into the mobile client.

Accessing Data Collection

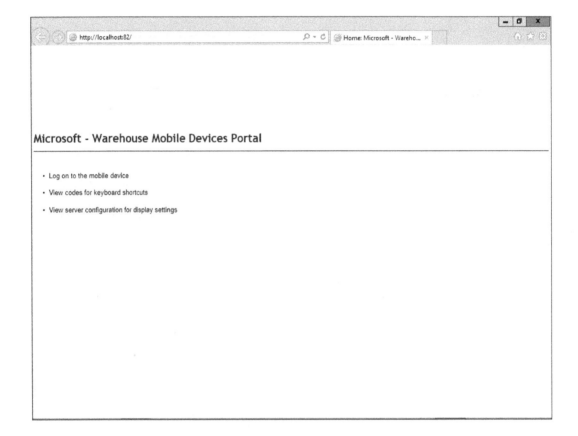

To do this, open up a web browser and browse to the **Mobile Device Portal**. If you are using the default install then it will probably be http://*servername*:82.

When the splash page is displayed, click on the **Log On To Mobile Device** hyperling.

Accessing Data Collection

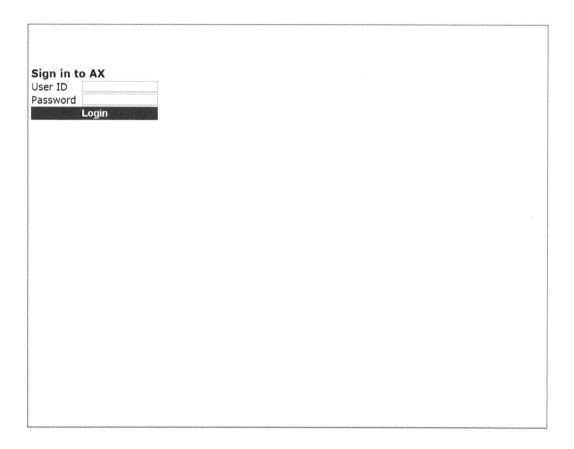

This will bring you to the **Sign In** form.

Accessing Data Collection

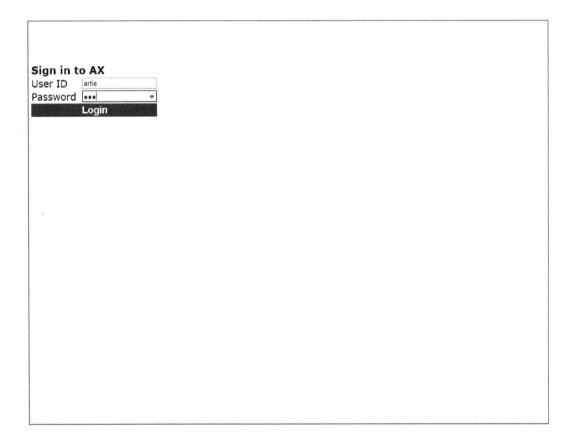

Just type in your username and password for WMS and click the **Login** button.

Accessing Data Collection

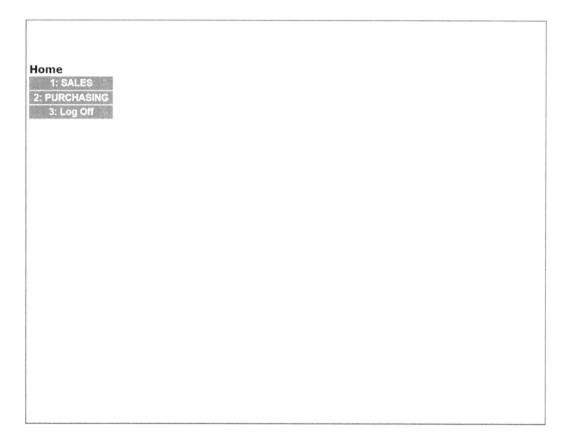

That will take you straight to the main menu that you associated with the user.

Rock on!

RECEIVING THROUGH WAREHOUSE MANAGEMENT

Now that we have everything up and running we can start running through some of the transactions using the Mobile Client. To start off we will show how you can receive and put away products.

Performing A PO Receipt Through Warehouse Management

The first task that we will perform is the PO Receipt operation.

Performing A PO Receipt Through Warehouse Management

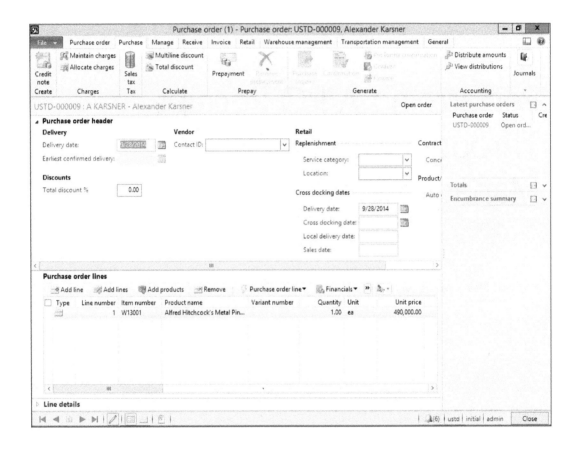

Start off by creating a Purchase Order that we want to receive.

Accessing Data Collection

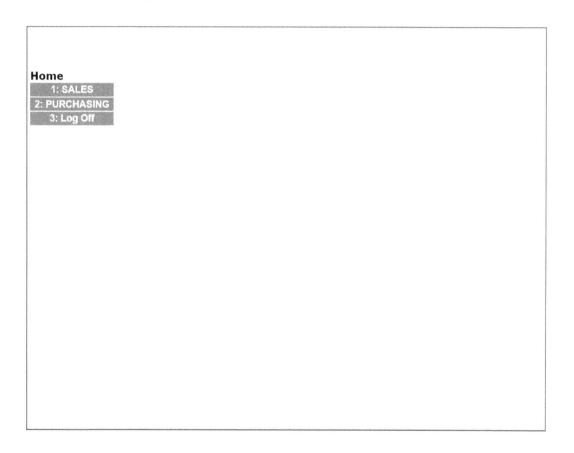

Then log into the mobile client and then click on the **PURCHASING** menu item.

Performing A PO Receipt Through Warehouse Management

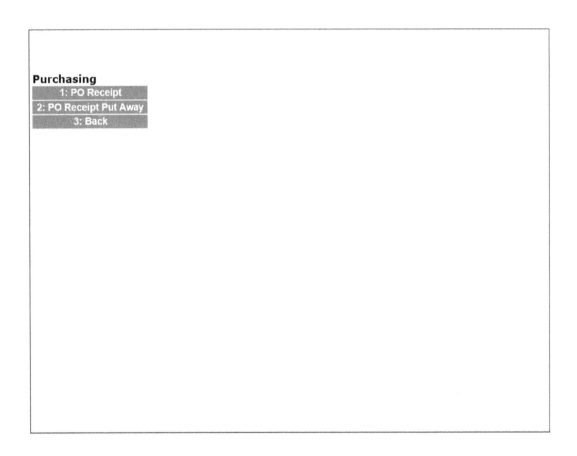

This will take you into the Purchasing sub-menu. Click on the **PO Receipt** menu item.

Performing A PO Receipt Through Warehouse Management

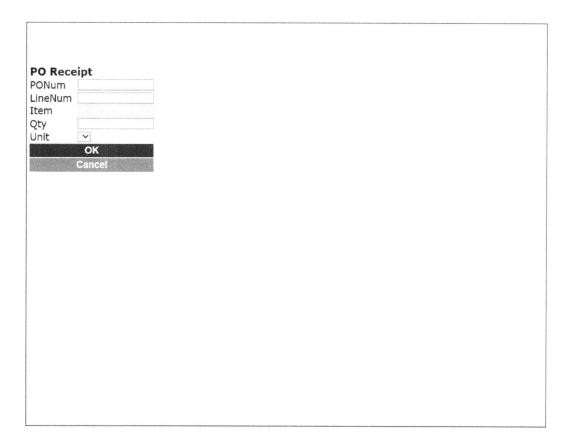

You will then be taken to the **PO Receipt** details.

Performing A PO Receipt Through Warehouse Management

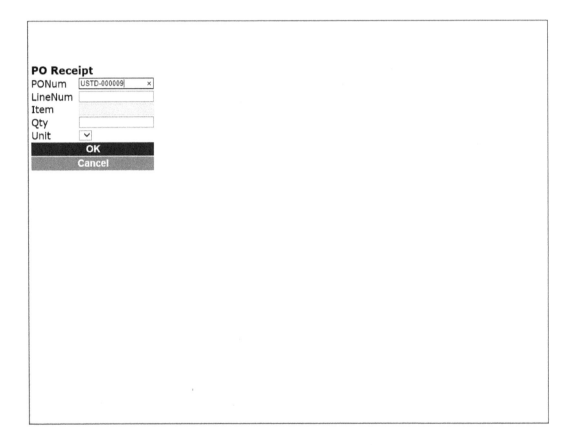

Enter (or scan) in the **PO Number** and press enter.

Performing A PO Receipt Through Warehouse Management

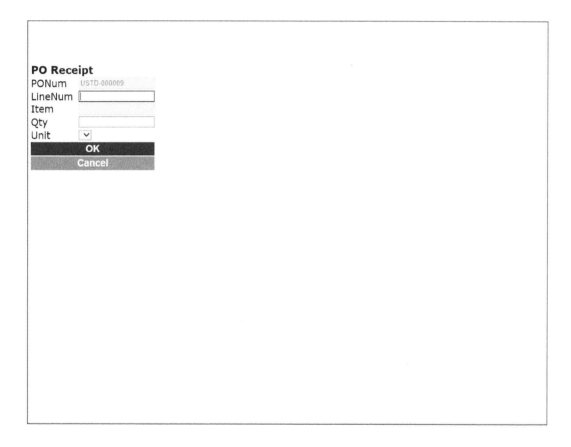

If the PO is valid you will be taken to the next line.

Performing A PO Receipt Through Warehouse Management

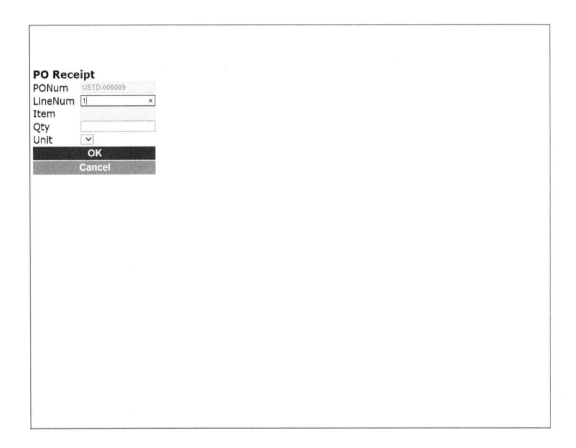

Type in the Line Number and then press enter.

Performing A PO Receipt Through Warehouse Management

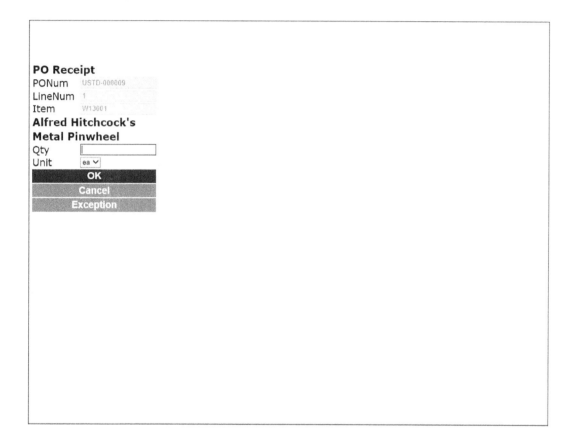

If the line number is valid then it will automatically show you the product code and also the descriptions from the product.

Performing A PO Receipt Through Warehouse Management

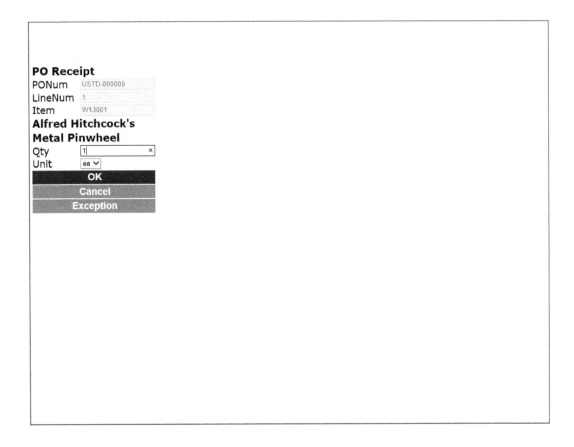

Now enter in the number of items that you are receiving and press enter.

Performing A PO Receipt Through Warehouse Management

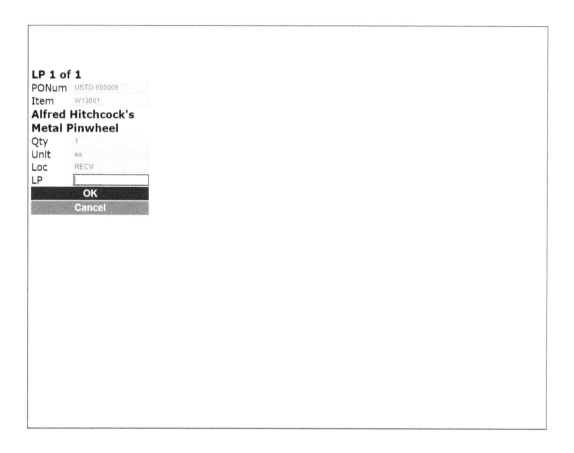

Because this is a license plate enabled product you now need to specify the License Plate.

Performing A PO Receipt Through Warehouse Management

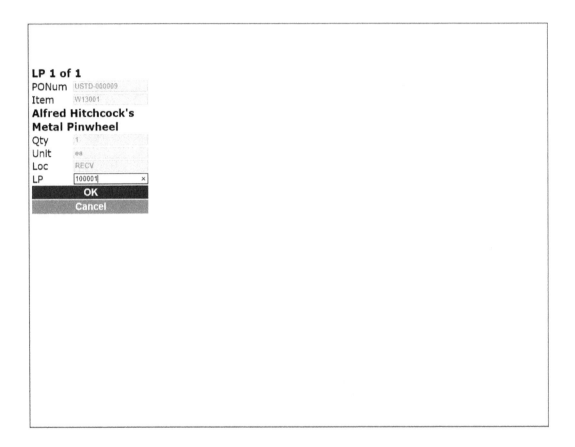

Enter in the tracking License Plate and press enter.

Performing A PO Receipt Through Warehouse Management

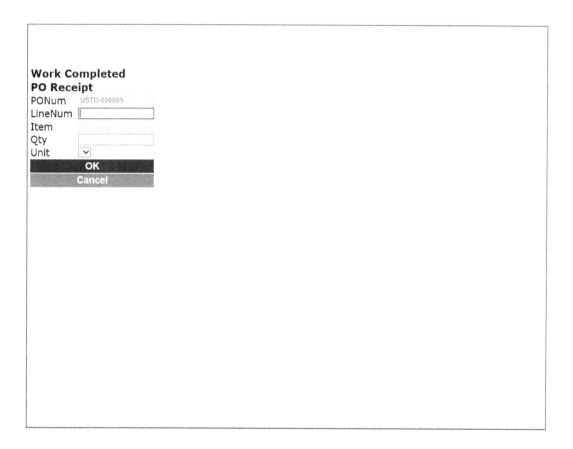

That completes the receipt of the product and you will be able to repeat the process again to receive in all of the other products that you like.

After you are finished with the receiving, just click on the **Cancel** button.

Performing A PO Receipt Through Warehouse Management

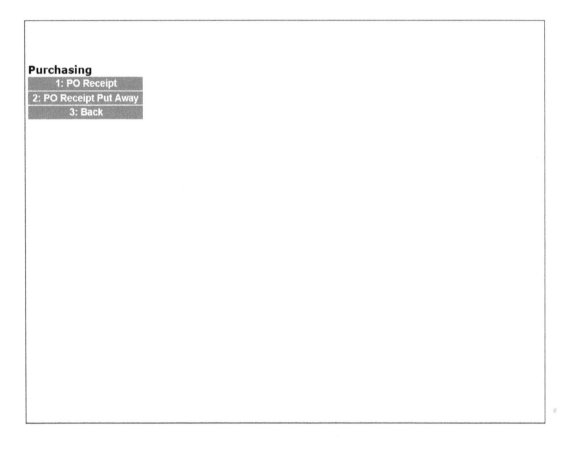

That will return you back to the **Purchasing** menu.

Viewing Received Inventory

Just to prove that there isn't any funny business going on, we will now check the inventory to see if the product was received.

Viewing Received Inventory

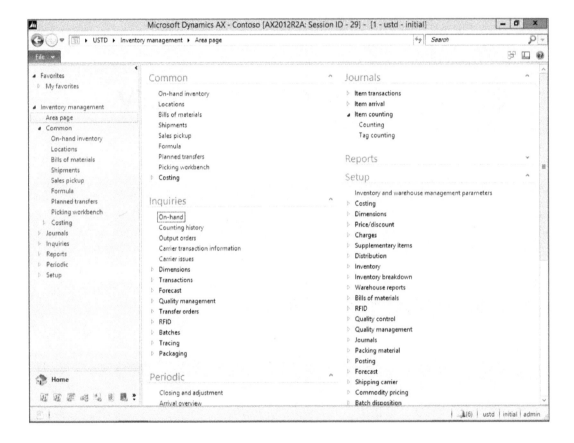

To do this, click on the **On-Hand** menu item within the **Inquiries** group of the **Inventory Management** area page.

Viewing Received Inventory

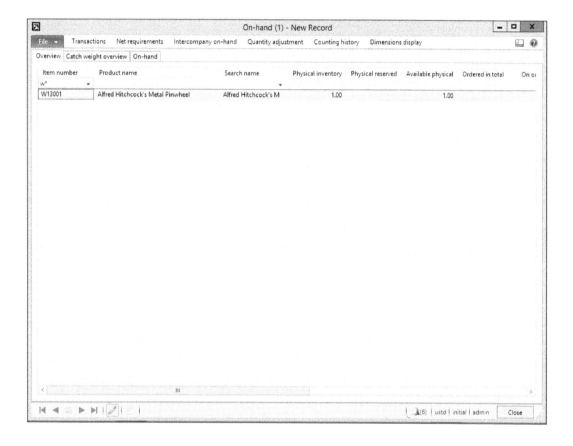

When the **On-Hand** inquiry is displayed, filter out the view to just the product and you will see that the product has been received.

Viewing Received Inventory

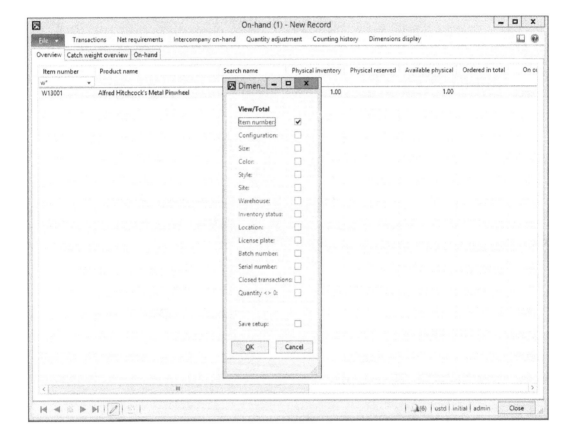

If you don't already see the license plate information then click on the **Dimension Display** button in the menu bar to pull up the dimension selector.

Viewing Received Inventory

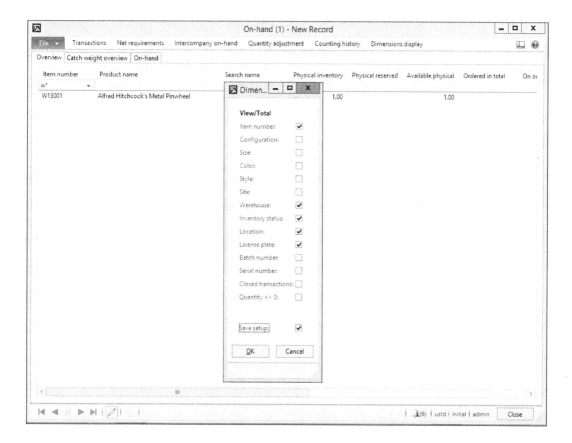

Check the **Warehouse**, **Inventory Status**, **Location**, and **License Plate** flags.

Then check the **Save Setup** flag before clicking on the **OK** button.

Viewing Received Inventory

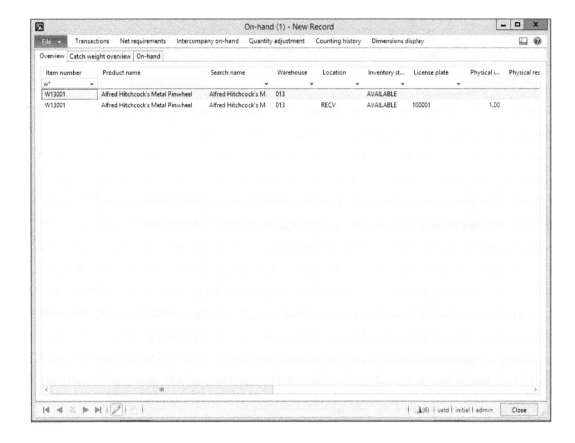

Now you can see that the product that we just received in is in the receiving area and also has a license plate associated to it.

Now click on the **Close** button to exit from the form.

Viewing Active Work

Since we have received in the product, this has created a work task for someone to put the product away. One way to see your work load is to view the active work screen within the system.

Viewing Active Work

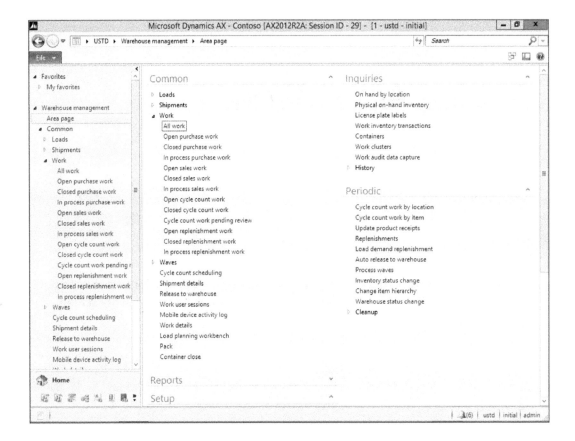

To do this click on the **All Work** menu item within the **Work** folder of the **Common** group within the **Warehouse Management** area page.

Viewing Active Work

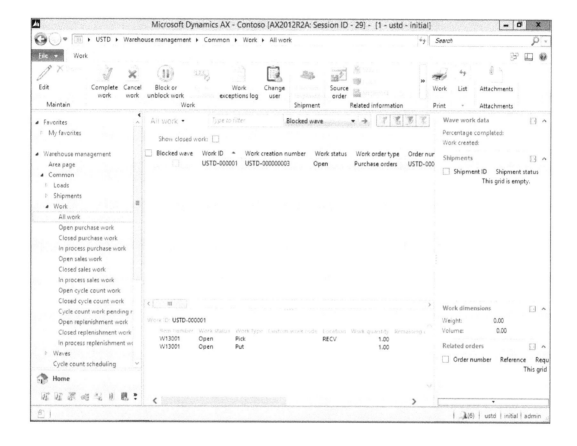

When the **All Work** list page is displayed you will see the work order that was created to put away the received product.

Printing Work Instructions

There are a number of different ways that you can assign work to people. If you want to do it the old fashioned way then you can just print out the work instruction.

Printing Work Instructions

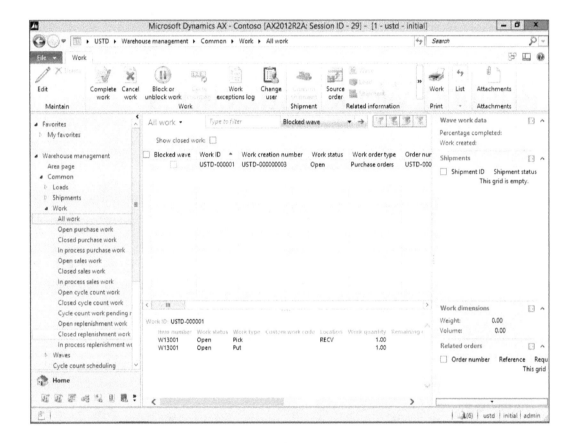

To do this return to the **All Work** list page, select the item that you want to print the work instructions for and then click no the **Work** button within the **Print** group of the **Work** ribbon bar.

Printing Work Instructions

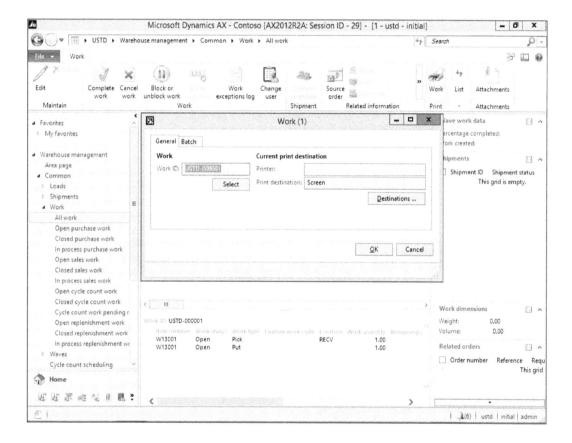

When the **Work** print dialog is displayed, just click on the **OK** button.

Printing Work Instructions

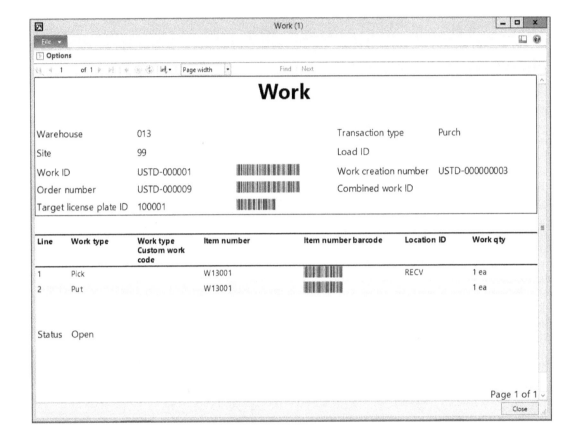

That will print out your work instructions for you.

Performing PO Putaway Through The Warehouse Management Client

Now that we have the work instructions we can have someone put the product away in the warehouse.

Performing PO Putaway Through The Warehouse Management Client

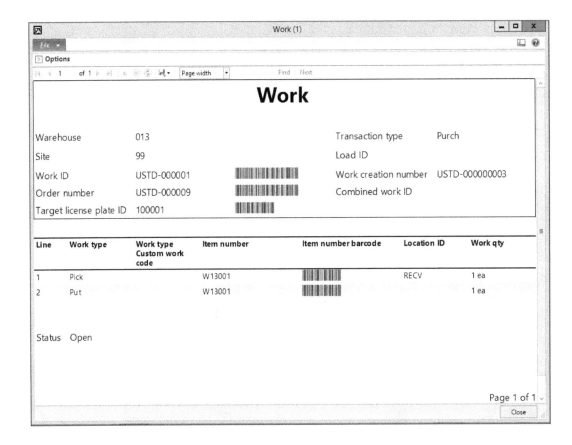

Remember that the Work Instructions are all bar coded so now you can just scan all of the information rather than type it in.

Performing PO Putaway Through The Warehouse Management Client

To do this, open up the Mobile Client, open up the **Purchasing** menu and click on the **PO Receipt Put Away** button.

Performing PO Putaway Through The Warehouse Management Client

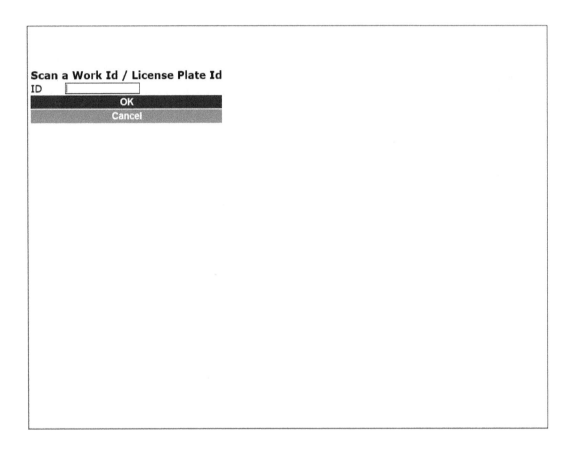

When this task opens it will ask you to type in a **Work ID** or a **License Plate** as a starting point for your work.

Performing PO Putaway Through The Warehouse Management Client

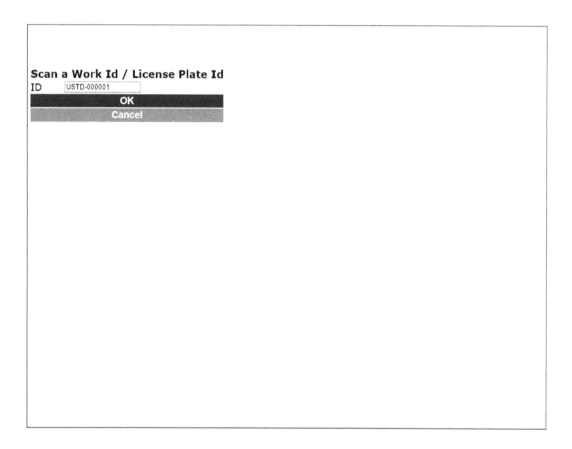

Scan in the **Work ID** and then press enter.

Performing PO Putaway Through The Warehouse Management Client

This will open up a summary of the Pick instructions including how much you need to puck and what you need to pick. If it all looks good then click on the **OK** button.

Performing PO Putaway Through The Warehouse Management Client

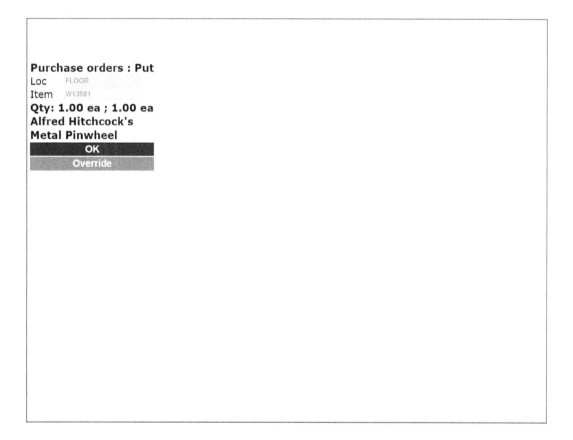

Because you have defined your Put Away directives it will suggest the Location to put the item and you can accept it just by clicking on the **OK** button.

Performing PO Putaway Through The Warehouse Management Client

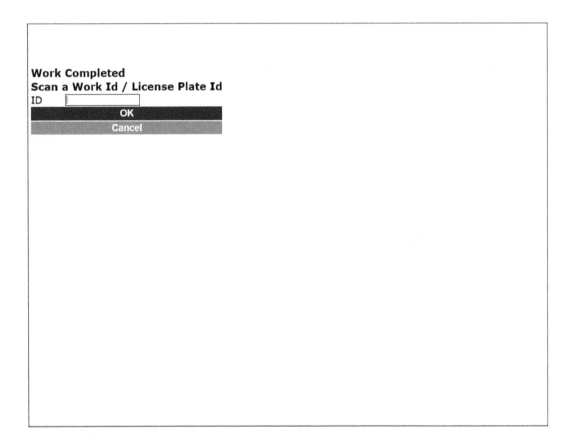

And you will be returned to the work order selection screen.

How easy was that?

PICKING & SHIPPING THROUGH WAREHOUSE MANAGEMENT

Once we have product in the warehouse we can sell it and that means that we need to perform a pick and ship operation through the handheld. In this section we will walk through the handheld transactions required to do this.

Configuring Load Templates

Before we start though there is just a little setup that we need to finish in the system. Since we are shipping the product we need to tell the system how are we loading the product, and that means that we need to create at least one **Load Template**.

Configuring Load Templates

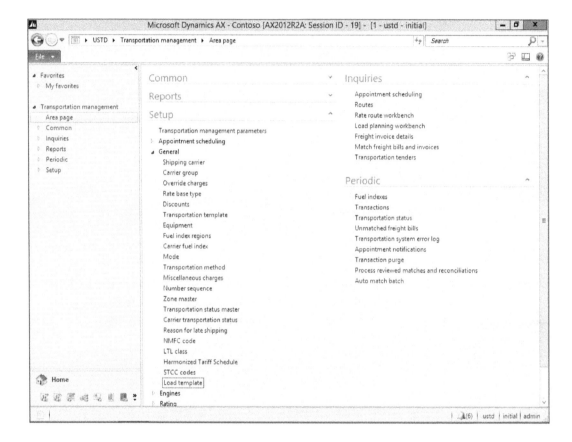

To do this, click on the **Load Templates** menu item within the **General** folder of the **Setup** group within the **Transportation Management** area page.

Configuring Load Templates

When the **Load Template** maintenance form is displayed, click on the **New** button within the menu bar to create a new record.

Configuring Load Templates

Set the **Load Template ID** to **LTL** and then click on the **Close** button to exit from the form.

Releasing Sales Orders To The Warehouse

Now we can start releasing sales orders to the shipping area.

Releasing Sales Orders To The Warehouse

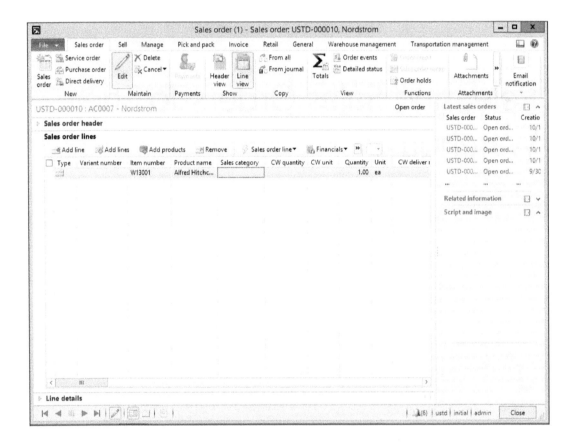

To do this start off with a Sales Order that you want to pick and ship.

Releasing Sales Orders To The Warehouse

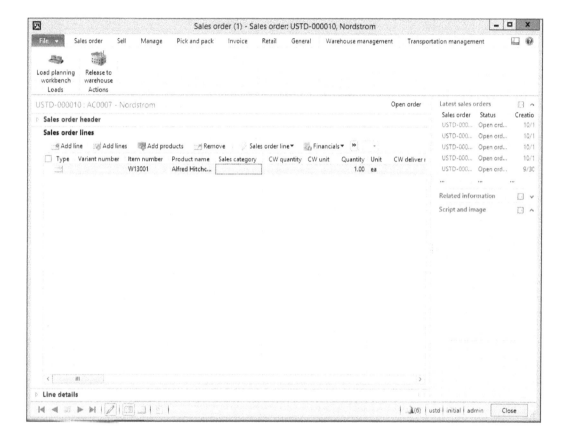

Then click on the **Release To Warehouse** button within the **Actions** group of the **Warehouse Management** ribbon bar to mark the order as ready for staging.

Releasing Sales Orders To The Warehouse

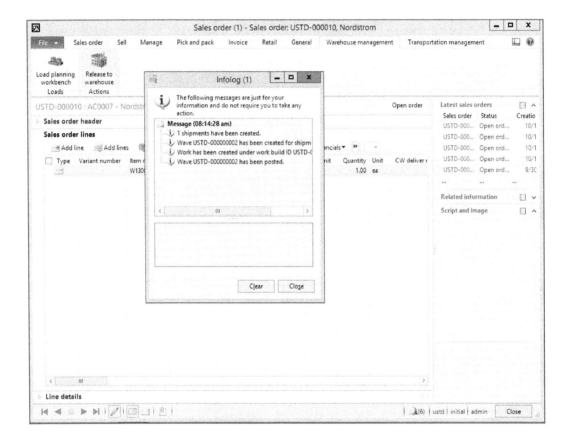

If everything is configured then you will get a notice from the system that a work order has been created, and you can exit out of the forms.

Viewing Shipment Work Details

Now that the work has been created we can view all of the shipment details.

Viewing Shipment Work Details

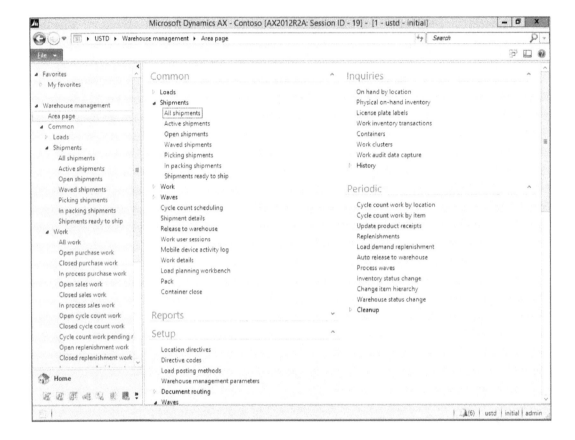

To do this, click on the **All Shipments** menu item within the **Shipments** folder of the **Common** group within the **Warehouse Management** area page.

Viewing Shipment Work Details

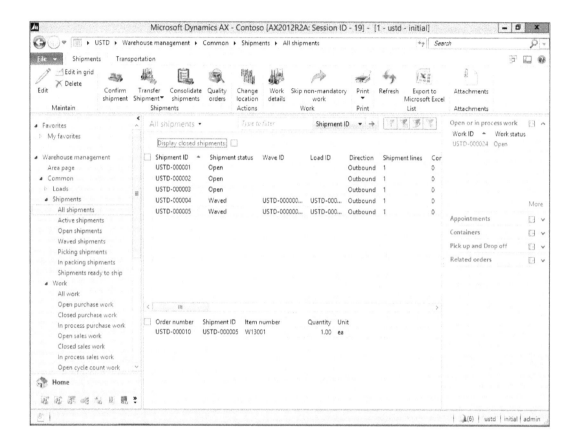

When the **All Shipments** list page is displayed, you will see that a shipment with work has been created as well.

Viewing Shipment Work Details

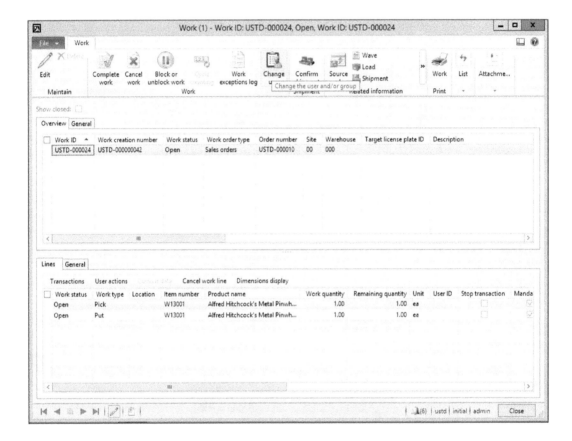

If you drill into the work details then you will be able to see that the pick and put instructions have been created for the shipment.

Picking Inventory Using The Warehouse Management Client

Now that we have released the order to the warehouse we can use the work instructions to get the product from the warehouse and bring it to the staging area.

Picking Inventory Using The Warehouse Management Client

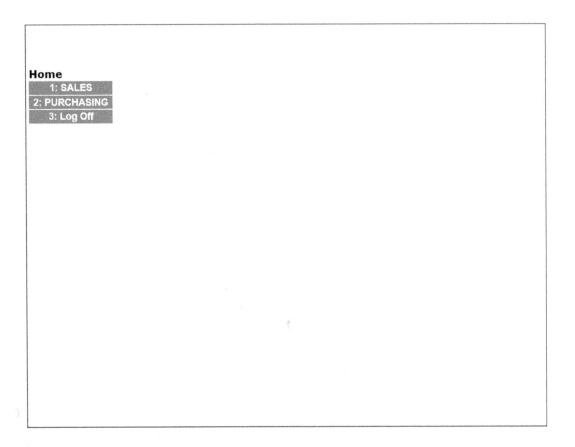

To do this, open up the Mobile Client and click on the **SALES** menu item.

Picking Inventory Using The Warehouse Management Client

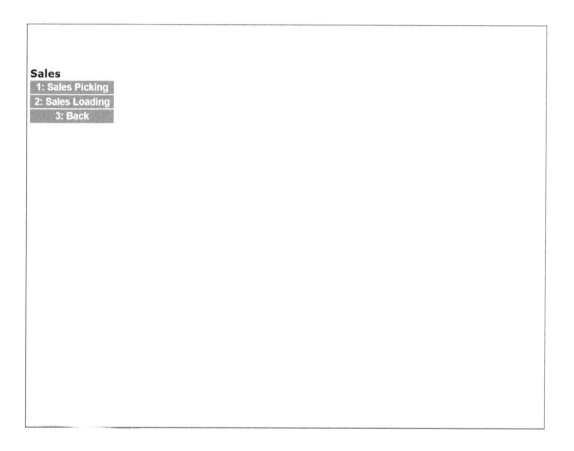

This will take you to the **Sales** menu where you can click on the **Sales Picking** menu item.

Picking Inventory Using The Warehouse Management Client

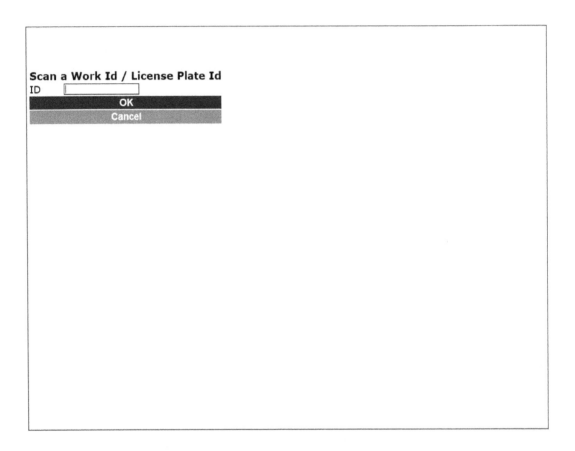

Since this is a work directed task you will be asked for your **Work ID**.

Picking Inventory Using The Warehouse Management Client

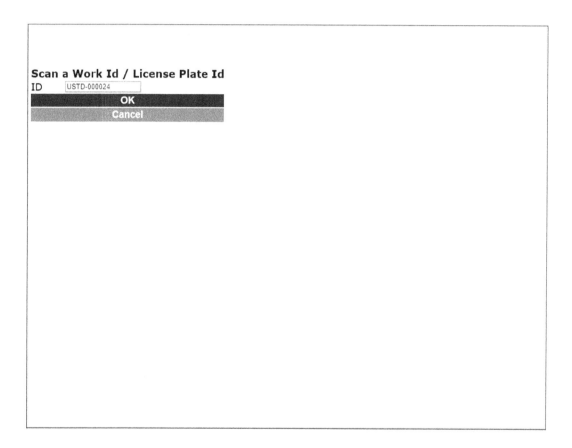

Scan in the **Work ID** and press enter.

Picking Inventory Using The Warehouse Management Client

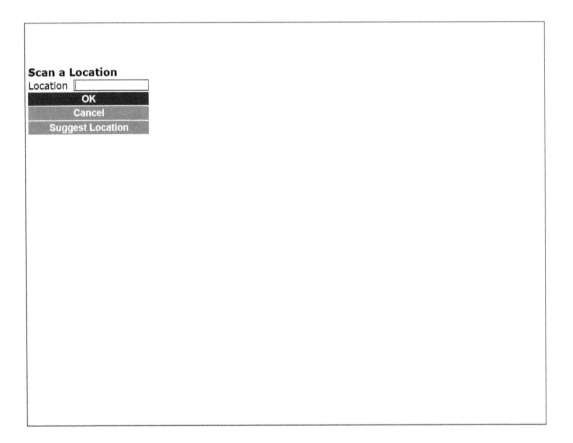

Although you are directed to the location that you want to pick the product from you do have the option to pick it from somewhere else, and will be asked for the location.

Picking Inventory Using The Warehouse Management Client

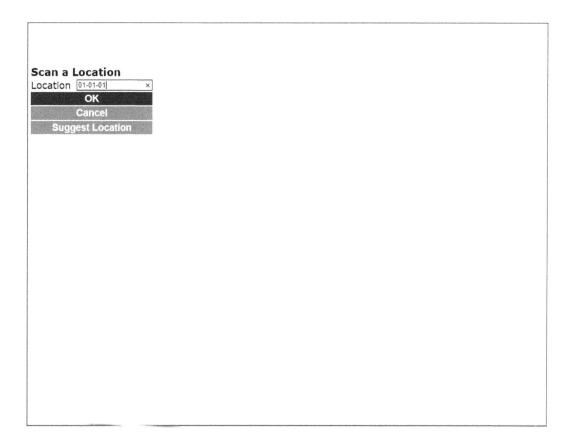

Scan in the location that you are picking the product from and then press enter.

Picking Inventory Using The Warehouse Management Client

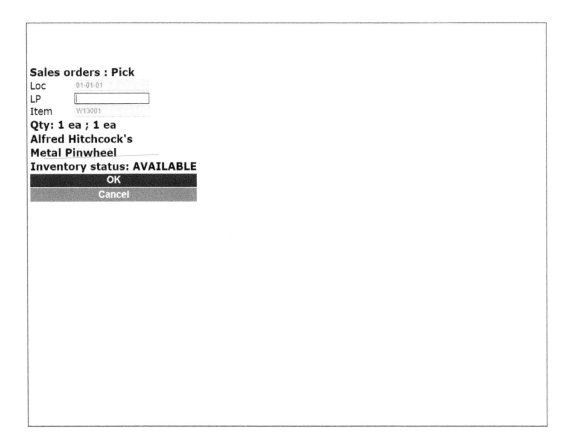

If the product is in the location then you will be asked to enter in the License Plate for the product that you are picking.

Picking Inventory Using The Warehouse Management Client

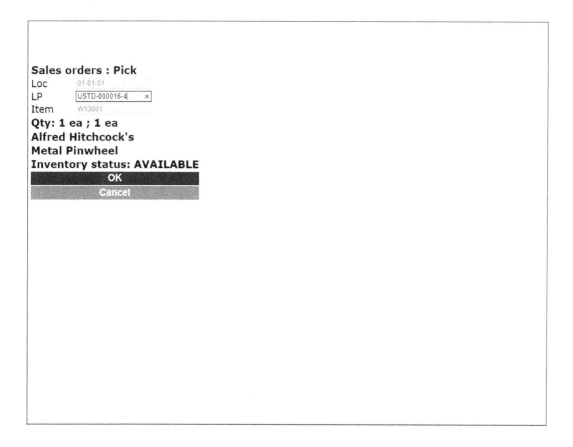

Scan in the license plate and then press enter.

Picking Inventory Using The Warehouse Management Client

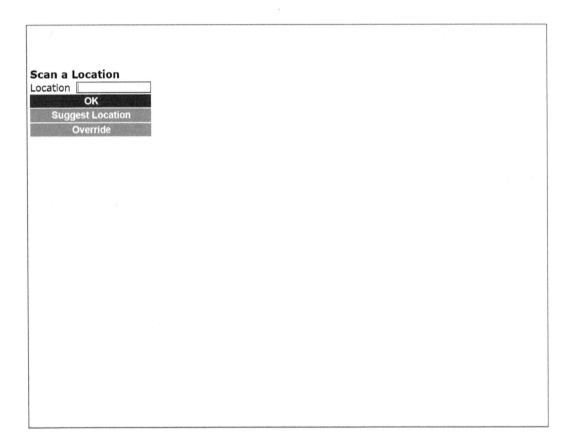

Once you have picked the product you will be asked where do you want to put it.

Picking Inventory Using The Warehouse Management Client

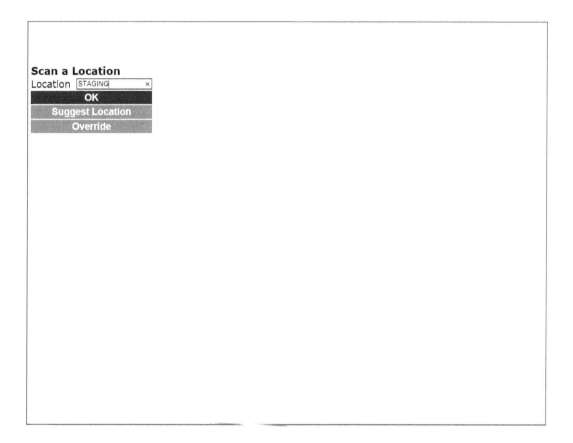

Scan in the **STAGING** location and press enter.

Picking Inventory Using The Warehouse Management Client

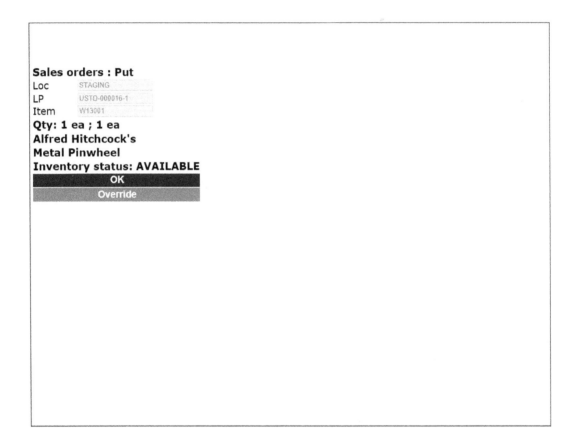

Then you will get a confirmation of the put. If everything looks good then just click on the **OK** button.

Picking Inventory Using The Warehouse Management Client

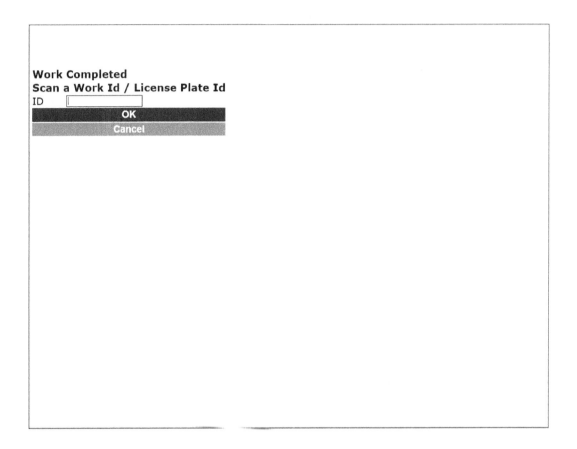

That will return you to the **Work ID** form where you can perform another pick.

Picking Inventory Using The Warehouse Management Client

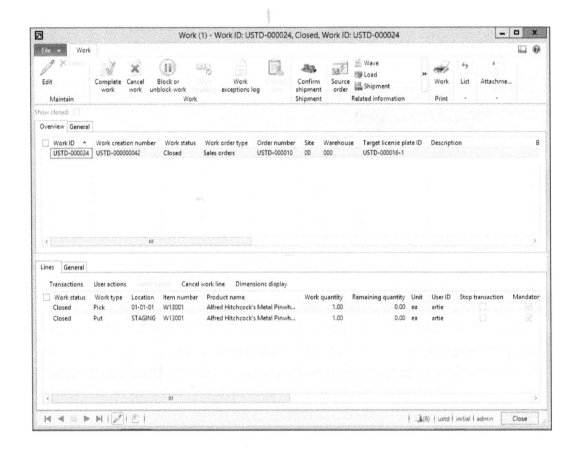

If you look at the work that was created for the pick you will see where the product was picked from and where you put it.

Very cool.

Confirming The Shipment

Now that the product has been staged, we can ship it out.

Confirming The Shipment

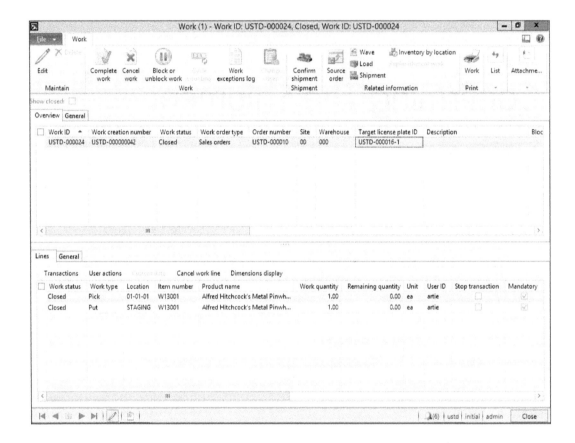

A quick way to do this is to open up the Work that was created for the shipment and click on the **Confirm Shipment** button within the **Shipment** group of the **Work** ribbon bar.

Confirming The Shipment

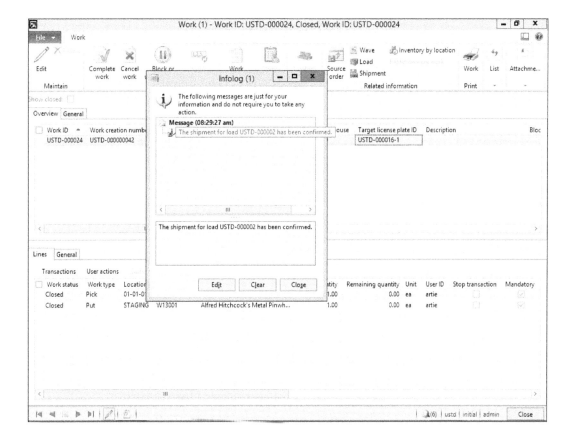

You should get a notice that the shipment has been loaded.

Viewing Shipments

Just to make sure that everything has been shipped we will take a quick peek at the shipments.

Viewing Shipments

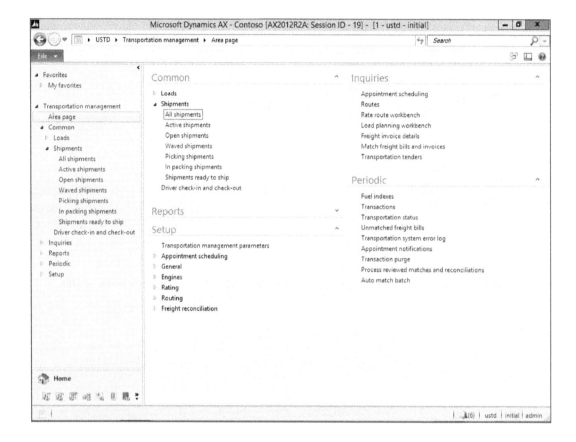

To do this, click on the **All Shipments** menu item within the **Shipments** folder of the **Common** group within the **Transportation Management** area page.

Viewing Shipments

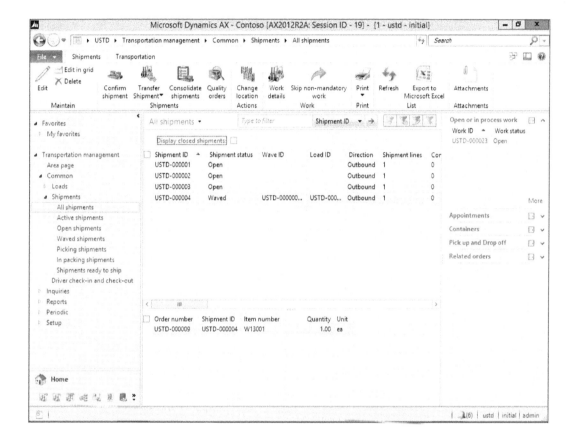

When the **All Shipments** list page is displayed you will probably notice that the shipment that you just confirmed is not there.

Viewing Shipments

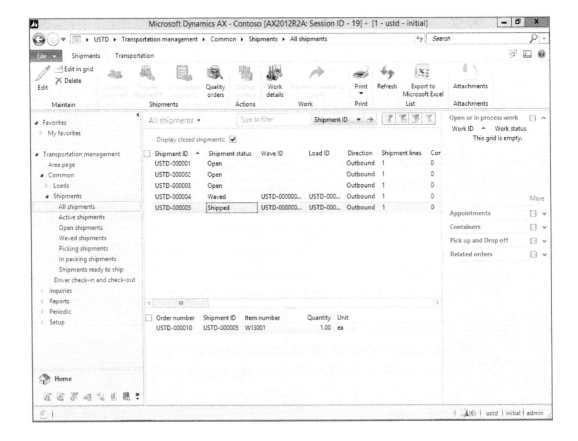

If you check the **Display Closed Shipments** flag in the header then you will see your lost shipment and see that it has been shipped.

How easy is that?

SUMMARY

Hopefully this book has given you an understanding of some of the basic functions of the Warehouse Management module within Dynamics AX, and also has shown you that it's really not that hard to configure. Don't get me wrong, it is a little bit more work than the standard Inventory module to configure, but the efficiencies that you can gain from spending just a little more time setting up your warehousing model will pay off in the end.

Now that you have mastered the basics of the Warehouse Management module, let it sink in for a little bit and then try to see what else you can do. There are a lot more functions that you can enable through the mobile device including Cycle Counting, and on demand counts and also you can start to refine your picking and put directives to be more clever within the warehouse.

You will be surprised at what more you can do with this module.

Want More Tips & Tricks For Dynamics AX?

The Tips & Tricks series is a compilation of all the cool things that I have found that you can do within Dynamics AX, and are also the basis for my Tips & Tricks presentations that I have been giving for the AXUG, and online. Unfortunately book page size restrictions mean that I can only fit 50 tips & tricks per book, but I will create new volumes every time I reach the 50 Tip mark.

To get all of the details on this series, then here is the link:

http://dynamicsaxcompanions.com/tipsandtricks

Need More Help With Dynamics AX?

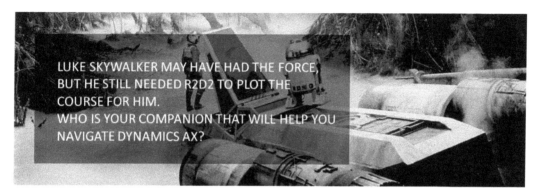

LUKE SKYWALKER MAY HAVE HAD THE FORCE,
BUT HE STILL NEEDED R2D2 TO PLOT THE
COURSE FOR HIM.
WHO IS YOUR COMPANION THAT WILL HELP YOU
NAVIGATE DYNAMICS AX?

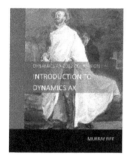
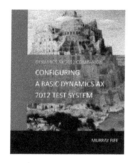

After creating a number of my walkthroughs on SlideShare showing how to configure the different areas within Dynamics AX, I had a lot of requests for the original documents so that people could get a better view of many of the screen shots and also have a easy reference as they worked through the same process within their own systems. To make them easier to access, I am in the process of moving all of the content to the Dynamics AX Companions website to easier access. If you are looking for details on how to configure and use Dynamics AX, then this is a great place for you to start.

Here is the link for the site:

http://dynamicsaxcompanions.com/

About Me

I am an author - I'm no Dan Brown but my books do contain a lot of secret codes and symbols that help guide you through the mysteries of Dynamics AX.

I am a curator - gathering all of the information that I can about Dynamics AX and filing it away within the Dynamics AX Companions archives.

I am a pitchman - I am forever extolling the virtues of Dynamics AX to the unwashed masses convincing them that it is the best ERP system in the world.

I am a Microsoft MVP - this is a big deal, there are less than 10 Dynamics AX MVP's in the US, and less than 30 worldwide.

I am a programmer - I know enough to get around within code, although I leave the hard stuff to the experts so save you all from my uncommented style.

WEB	**www.**murrayfife.me
EMAIL	murray@dynamicsaxcompanions.com
TWITTER	@murrayfife
SKYPE	murrayfife
AMAZON	www.amazon.com/author/murrayfife
WEB	www.dynamicsaxcompanions.com